The Elizabethan Theatre II

The Elizabethan Theatre II

Papers given at the Second International
Conference on Elizabethan Theatre held at the
University of Waterloo, Ontario, in July 1969

Edited and with an introduction by
DAVID GALLOWAY
Department of English,
University of New Brunswick

Published in collaboration with the
University of Waterloo

Archon Books

1970

Acknowledgments

In acknowledging the help which I have received, not only in the editing of this book but in the organizing and running of the Conference out of which the book has grown, I run the risk of tedious repetition, because all those people who helped with the first Conference of 1968, and who were still available, helped with the second Conference of 1969. This continuing support did much to ensure a conference of high quality, and showed a commendable spirit of harmony among the workers.

For the second year running the Conference was made possible by the financial support of the Canada Council and the University of Waterloo, and those in the higher echelons of the university's administrative Chain of Being – H. E. Petch, Acting President, J. S. Minas, Acting Academic Vice-President, and W. U. Ober, Acting Dean of Arts – unobtrusively helped to smooth the way. David Hedges, the Assistant Director of the Conference, calmly gave invaluable help in nearly all phases of the operation and, once more, Fr. J. R. Finn, President of the University of St. Jerome's College, allowed us to savour something of the delights of the Mermaid Tavern. The running of the Conference was again largely in the hands of a dedicated and capable group of graduate students. Mrs. Johanna Hanson and Mrs. Shirley Thomson dealt with the registration and much of the general administration; Mrs. Betty McCutchan and Miss Edith Rice acted as chauffeurs far beyond the call of duty; and Mr. Lee Owen, assisted by his wife Laura, spent long hours looking after the bar. Mrs. Evelyn Gair of the University of New Brunswick prepared the index for this book.

I am especially indebted to the Macmillan Company of Canada which, in agreeing to the publication of these papers in advance, gave the contributors the added lure of a more permanent and widespread audience than the Conference could supply. I am particularly grateful to Mrs. Diane Mew, Executive Editor, College

Acknowledgments

Department, who, of course, bore the brunt of the editorial problems involved in preparing the book for the press, and for the reassuring presence of Mr. Pat Meany – a true friend of scholarship.

D.G.

Contents

Introduction

In writing an introduction to a book such as this an editor can seek – perhaps desperately – for certain unifying themes, or he can throw in his hand and say that "every paper speaks for itself." The subject matter of most of the papers printed here has much in common, but it would be protesting too much to suggest that, as a whole, they represent a sustained treatment of a homogeneous body of material.

The scholarly emphasis of the First International Conference, held at the University of Waterloo in July 1968, was on the structure of certain "Elizabethan" theatres; the emphasis in this book – the papers delivered at the Second International Conference in July 1969 – is on the dramatic companies, their organization, their personnel, and their repertories. A successful conference is, however, much more than the sum of its papers, and I can only repeat what I wrote a year ago: "What is not represented here is its other dimension – the valuable formal and informal discussions in a friendly, intimate yet professional atmosphere." Largely as a result of J. A. Lavin's paper, much of the Conference discussion in fact centred on the question of the inductive method and the validity of generalizations about dramatic companies and theatres – a discussion for which all the papers, in varying degrees, provided a basis.

In the first paper, "Shakespeare and Jonson: Fact and Myth," S. Schoenbaum deals with the two giants, and the opinions of their contemporaries about them. He discusses various seventeenth, eighteenth and nineteenth century traditions about the relationships between the two men (most of which are more picturesque than factual), exorcises many of the "old ghosts" which haunt biography and criticism, and tries to "restore the picture, overlaid with the dust of centuries, of two excellent playwrights who sometimes laboured for the same company, and who took a lively interest in one another's work" (p. 18). Shadowy as the relationship between Shakespeare and Jonson remains to twentieth-century eyes, "we may rest assured that Heminge and Condell would not have invited Jonson to contribute the principal eulogy of the First Folio if he were not their fellow's friend, and Jonson would not have penned so noble a tribute if he did not esteem Shakespeare as an artist and treasure him as a comrade. Nor would he have, in the privacy of his study, described Shakespeare with a warmth that he expressed for no other poet. We may believe that he loved the man; to be sure, on this side idolatry" (p. 18).

In the second paper, "The Children of Paul's, 1551-1582," Trevor Lennam adds to our knowledge of the career of Sebastian Westcott, discusses the composition and repertory of his company of boys, and cautiously suggests hitherto unproposed sites for his playhouse. Professor Lennam, while admitting that "the precise location of the Paul's playhouse remains obscure" (p. 28), rejects the almonry house, the hall of the college of Minor Canons, St. Gregory's Church and the Chapter or Convocation House, and sees, as more likely sites, either eight tenements in Carter Lane between Sermon and Dolittle Lanes, or a "hospitio and tenement" fronting Paternoster Row at the entrance to Paul's Alley (see p. 32).

Continuing the story of the boys' companies, but from a different point of view than Professor Lennam's, R. A. Foakes, in "Tragedy at the Childrens' Theatres after 1600: A Challenge to the Adult Stage," feels that the importance of the experiments in the boys' theatres needs to be emphasized more strongly. He suggests that Alfred Harbage's picture of "two rival traditions, each throwing up a homogeneous body of drama, and each opposed to the other" (p. 38), needs to be considerably modified. Rather, he says, "the revival of the childrens' theatres in 1599/1600 soon made a great impact on the London theatre as a whole, and challenged the adult stages strongly enough to force them to take over and use in their own way styles and techniques of drama first exploited in the plays put on by the boys; . . . the children's theatres and the dramatists who wrote for them formed a major influence in determining the course English drama was to take" (p. 39).

While in a sense D. F. Rowan's paper, "A Neglected Jones/Webb Theatre Project, Part II: A Theatrical Missing Link," arising from his discovery of the Jones/Webb drawings at Worcester College,

Oxford, in March 1969, belongs more fittingly to the proceedings of the First Conference, it warrants inclusion in this volume because of its importance *per se* and because it is naturally related to his paper on "The Cockpit-in-Court" in *Elizabethan Theatre [I]*. If we accept Professor Rowan's arguments that the drawings represent a "missing link" between an early public theatre (The Swan) and a later court theatre (The Cockpit-in-Court), we have impressive evidence for a continuum of theatre practice and design from the 1590s to the 1630s. The implications of the discovery will have to be weighed carefully, but whether or not we accept his arguments about provenance and date, the drawings will have to be taken into account in future studies of the Elizabethan, Jacobean and Caroline theatres.

J. A. Lavin's paper, "The Elizabethan Theatre and the Inductive Method," delivers a timely onslaught on the misuse of the inductive method by historians of the "Elizabethan" theatre. Drawing much of his ammunition from D. F. McKenzie's attack on bibliographers in his article, "Printers of the Mind: Some Notes on Bibliographical Theories and Printing-House Practices," in *Studies in Bibliography*, XXII (1969), Professor Lavin sees "the inductive method lurking" in the work of scholars such as Richard Hosley, Alfred Harbage and Irwin Smith, and concludes that "attempts to generalize about Elizabethan theatres, acting, dramatic companies and theatrical texts are at the best naive, and at the worst positively misleading" (p. 86).

As if in defiance of Professor Lavin's warnings, Lise-Lone Marker's paper, "Nature and Decorum in the Theory of Elizabethan Acting," takes a broad view of "Elizabethan" acting techniques, and sees the Elizabethan actor as having a much more homogeneous style than Professor Lavin, and perhaps many others, would allow. Professor Marker draws on works as widely separated chronologically as Abraham Fraunce's *The Arcadian Rhetorique* (1588), Thomas Wright's *The Passions of the Mind* (1604) and John Bulwer's *Pathemyotomia* (1649), and suggests an acting style that changes little in over half a century and which owes much to earlier acting traditions. Classical views on the art of acting, for example, permeate Hamlet's instructions to the players and "the classical belief that Nature consists of absolute forms which the artist is capable of imitating, as he proceeds in presenting active counterparts of truth through his particular medium, provides the broad foundation for an entire tradition of acting that was ultimately swept away by naturalism" (pp. 89-90).

In the last paper of the formal sessions of the Conference, it was appropriate, perhaps, that Bernard Beckerman should remind us that the play's the thing in his discussion of *Measure for Measure* – one of the plays which, together with *Hamlet* and *The Alchemist*, members of the Conference went to see at Stratford, Ontario. In "A Shakespearean Experiment: The Dramaturgy of *Measure for Measure*," Professor Beckerman analyses the skill with which Shakespeare constructs this "flawed masterpiece," concludes that the dramatist "sought to create a peculiar type of tragicomedy," and that "the intrigue of the second half, essentially comedic, was designed to purge the essentially tragic passion of the first" (p. 132). The play, however, "culminates in a *tour de force* of discovery that is both a theatrical delight and an object lesson. By correctly identifying the weaknesses and by deeply appreciating Shakespeare's artistic intent, we can better place both halves of the play in proper dramatic balance and find those stage moments that will fulfill Shakespeare's experiment in tragicomedy" (p. 133).

Just when we had thought that the serious part of the Conference was over, and when Peter Davison was singing some Shakespearean burlesques at the dinner on the last night, the inductive method reared its head again when he broke off – in mid-stanza as it were – to call attention to D. F. McKenzie's article once more. To Mr. McKenzie's "salutary reminders" Mr. Davison delivered "salutary reminders" and, in "Marry, Sweet Wag," he argues that the article, "despite its many qualities . . . appeared to be based on a misunderstanding of humanistic enquiry" (p. 134). Mr. Davison asserts that "bibliography attempts to work with two of the most worthwhile and most perplexing of variables: human beings and literature," and that "the laws of logic apply to neither" (p. 143). But "we must continue to strive to push back the moment when we have to make our conjectures – when the guessing must begin – and we ought to be careful when we guess, that our guesses do do not slip into seeming facts; but it is surely farcical to imagine, after nearly 3,000 years of unsuccessful inquiring, that the exposure of further errors over procedures will cause the human urge to discover, to guess what an author meant, to suddenly wither and die" (p. 143).

The debate on the validity of the inductive method will, no doubt, continue, but this book is no mere part of a "grand remonstrance"; the scholarship in it outweighs the polemics of methodology.

Labels such as "Elizabethan" and "Victorian," by their continuing use, seem to impose, in the words of G. M. Young, "an illusory show of continuity and uniformity on a tract of time where men and manners, science and philosophy, the fabric of social life and its directing ideas" are changing rapidly. Professor Foakes, in fact, mentions the period of revolutionary change which occurred on the London stage in the 1950s, to remind us that "the further back we travel mentally in time, the greater the effort of imagination required to realize that a span of ten years is a long time to those living through it, and may seem to them full of novelty and change. Distinctions tend to dissolve, and changes go unnoticed, in the broad perspective of the Elizabethan and Jacobean stage" (p. 38). It is well that we are constantly reminded of such things, and if we must constantly try to answer Professor Lavin's questions – "What actor, what stage and when?" – we should also remember that the habits and training of youth can die hard, and that actors do not necessarily change their mannerisms and attitudes, their strengths and limitations, as they move from one theatre to another. Even the sweeping generalizations of some scholars can spur others to test those generalizations in further research.

Few scholars consistently and consciously follow inductive or deductive methods, and out of a mixture of both, many frustrations and some luck, their books are made.

Even if we agree with William Blake that "to Generalize is to be an Idiot," we should, presumably, not wish to reach the mental stalemate of Lord Acton's teacher, Johann von Döllinger, of whom Acton said, "He would not write with imperfect materials, and to him the materials were always imperfect."

David Galloway
Department of English
University of New Brunswick

The Elizabethan Theatre II

Shakespeare and Jonson:
Fact and Myth

S. SCHOENBAUM

It is one of the curiosities of literary scholarship that the twentieth century, already two-thirds past, has not yet produced an authoritative biography of Shakespeare which synthesizes modern learning and reflects the modern temper. Chambers' two monumental volumes still dominate the scene, a mighty Everest, but although the author later referred to them as a "Life," they are better described by Chambers' own subtitle: *A Study of Facts and Problems.* That serious scholars should now shrink from attempting the authoritative biography which each age requires is understandable enough. The inadequacies of the documentary record are familiar to all. And how irritating that the traditions and legends which cluster together to form the Shakespeare mythos should show the author of *Lear* tippling with sots and greeting the dawn from beneath a crabtree's spreading canopy, poaching deer, and fornicating with an innkeeper's wife, but hardly ever reveal the supreme dramatist in the creative context of the London theatrical world. About his relations with his fellows we know little except that Heminge and Condell valued so worthy a friend, and Augustine Philips, that stalwart of the Chamberlain's Men, bequeathed him a thirty-shilling piece in gold. But what of Shakespeare's dealings with other playwrights? About this side of his professional life, rather than the acting, curiosity is after all most intense.

In his triple capacity – playwright, actor, shareholder – he must have often come into contact with other dramatists. If we can accept the conclusions of modern scholarship, Munday, Dekker, Chettle, and possibly Heywood called on him to help salvage a play, *Sir Thomas More*, that had run afoul of the censor. But the first three men nowhere allude to Shakespeare, and the last, Heywood, mentions him briefly and uninformatively on two occasions – he praises mellifluous Shakespeare, he complains that an unscrupulous printer has included two of his poems under Shakespeare's name in *The Passionate Pilgrim*. Fletcher succeeded Shakespeare as principal dramatist for the King's Men, and during the period of transition the two playwrights may have collaborated on *Henry VIII* and also on *The Two Noble Kinsmen;* yet the younger man nowhere records his impressions of the retiring master. Jonson remains; and it is fitting that we should glimpse in conjunction with one another the two colossi who bestrode the drama of the age.

I

Shakespeare and Jonson: how many themes for argument the linking of the two names conjures up! Focus on their writings, and we may see them as representatives, the greatest in their day, of mutually exclusive conceptions of the playwright's craft: romantic versus classical, nature versus art, the theatre of a whole people versus the theatre of a côterie. These are subjects for whole papers, and indeed have been much discussed. The biographical side, however, has commanded least attention of late, and so I shall dwell on that.

For the relations between Shakespeare and Jonson, personal and professional, we have a number of records, and these are supplemented by a body of traditionary lore. But knowledge, no less than ignorance, brings its problems. What manner of coexistence obtained between the two giants of the Elizabethan stage? Were they friends, genial rivals, or adversaries? Shall we in the mind's eye see them feasting and carousing and exchanging happy specimens of tavern wit? Or shall we imagine the fell incensed points of mighty opposites towering above baser natures? Both these conceptions, as well as various intermediary gradations, are available to us. As specialists whose task it is to seek the truth, we are confronted not only with the evidence but also with a scholarly tradition which has, over the centuries, made a critical battleground of the subject, generating heat and passion and, rather less often, shedding light. It behoves us at times to examine our scholarly heritage. Such an exercise will yield consoling instances of the fallibility of our betters and furnish edifying *exempla* of the dangers of interpretation; it may also help us to achieve that sense of historical perspective which can enable us to steer clear of prejudice and to resolve contradictions.

First a word about the records. I shall, I fear, be traversing some well-ploughed terrain, but better to do so than to falsify the picture by omission; and sometimes a fresh look even at the familiar brings its rewards, not the least of these being the elimination of hereditary confusions.

In the Jonson Folio of 1616 Shakespeare's name heads the list of "principall Comoedians" in *Every Man in His Humour*, and also appears prominently among the "principall Tragoedians" who acted *Sejanus*. To the First Folio of 1623 Jonson contributed not only his celebrated eulogy of Shakespeare but also the verse accompanying the Droeshout engraving. To my mind a mood of affectionate warmth pervades these poems: we hear of "my beloued," "Soul of the Age," "my gentle Shakespeare," "Sweet Swan of Auon." The actors had praised him for never blotting a line, but Jonson insists that his friend (like himself) did sweat and "strike the second heat / Upon the Muses anuile," and he goes on to praise

> his well torned, and true filed lines:
> In each of which, he seemes to shake a Lance,
> As brandish't at the eyes of Ignorance.

An odd way of viewing Shakespeare's accomplishment, to be accounted for by the irresistible Elizabethan urge to pun, which Jonson displays elsewhere in his occasional poems by his quibbles upon the names Portland, Palmer, and Brome. Perhaps, however, it is not entirely fanciful to discern the author's identification with his subject: these lines apply more aptly to Jonson than they do to Shakespeare, who wages no campaigns against ignorance. Self-congratulation is the sincerest form of compliment. When not under encomiastic obligations, in notebooks that remained unpublished until after his death, Jonson affirms that he loved the man, and honours his memory on this side idolatry. "Hee was (indeed) honest, and of an open, and free nature: had an excellent *Phantsie*; brave notions, and gentle expressions. . . ." *Honest* is the most laudatory term in Jonson's lexicon of praise.

These remarks require no super-subtle reading. What evidence, from the record, for the opposing image of Jonson the calumniating rival? In his eulogy he speaks of Shakespeare's "small Latine, and Lesse Greeke," a phrase offensive to bardolatrous ears, but not necessarily patronizing. Jonson is more openly critical in his *Discoveries*, already cited: would Shakespeare had blotted a thousand lines! That way he might have avoided such inanities "As when hee said in the person of *Caesar*, one speaking to him; *Caesar thou dost me wrong*. Hee replyed: *Caesar did never wrong, but with just cause* and such like. . . ." The passage does not appear in *Julius Caesar* but a half line apparently marks the place of excision; perhaps Shakespeare heeded his friend's advice and deleted – not an absurdity, surely – but a penetrating paradox. Elsewhere Jonson alludes disparagingly to the *Henry VI* plays and to *Henry V*, to *Titus Andronicus*, *The Tempest*, and "mouldy tales" like *Pericles*. Drummond records Jonson's censure that "Shaksperr wanted Arte," and his jibe at the shipwreck in Bohemia, "wher y^r is no Sea near by some 100 Miles." In his *Essay on the Dramatique Poetry of the Last Age*, Dryden reports that Jonson threw up his hands in horror at some bombast speeches in *Macbeth*. Some have found an allusion to Shakespeare's motto in the one proposed by Puntarvolo for Sogliardo in *Every Man out of His Humour*: "Not without mustard"; others, however, find a favourable reference to Shakespeare as the second pen that had a good share in the stage version of *Sejanus*. But such allusions belong to the conjectural rather than the factual record and need not detain us.

About Jonson, as about all contemporary authors with the exception of the dead shepherd Marlowe and the Rival Poet (whoever *he* may be), Shakespeare is silent, but the University of Cambridge, around 1601, favours us with an intriguing anecdote. In the Second Part of *The Return from Parnassus*, performed at St. John's, Kempe informs us:

> Why heres our fellow *Shakespeare* puts them all downe, I and *Ben Ionson* too. O that *Ben Ionson* is a pestilent fellow, he brought vp *Horace* giuing the Poets a pill, but our fellow *Shakespeare* hath giuen him a purge that made him beray his credit.[1]

In time, commentators would make much of this purge and Shakespeare's triumph over Ben, naively failing to see that the praise in the *Parnassus* play is ironic; for the portrait of Kempe reflects the university scholar's scorn for an unlettered stage clown.

[1]*The Three Parnassus Plays*, ed. J. B. Leishman (1949), p. 337.

How shall we, who hopefully are not naive, evaluate the Shake-
speare-Jonson record? Let us begin with the *Parnassus* allusion. If
one may be allowed the collocation of metaphorical clichés, it has
started many hares but upon examination turns out to be a red
herring. Dekker, not Shakespeare, administered a purge to Jonson
in *Satiromastix*; perhaps, as is suggested by J. B. Leishman, the
able editor of the *Parnassus* trilogy, the anonymous university playwright thought of the Globe and the Chamberlain's Men as Shakespeare's theatre and Shakespeare's company: guilt by association.
Perhaps he was simply confused, for his information about the
London theatrical scene is otherwise not very precise; Kempe was
apparently no longer one of Shakespeare's fellows, having moved
to a rival company.[2] As for Jonson's remarks on Shakespeare as a
writer, these are such strictures as one might expect from a poet
who constructed his own art on very different principles; and one
must guard against confusing aesthetic with personal issues. I detect no malice in Jonson's comments, only the candour of one who
prided himself above all else on his honesty. As for Drummond, he
is the sort of man of whom you can say that if you have him for a
friend, then you don't need an enemy. If we can believe this hos-
tile witness, Jonson described Middleton as a base fellow, and
dismissed Sharpham, Day, and Minshew as rogues; he said that
Abraham Fraunce in his English hexameters was a fool and that
Donne, for not keeping accent, deserved hanging. But even in
Drummond, Jonson never refers to Shakespeare in such terms. So
far as Dryden's report is concerned, it comes late; the two men
could not have known one another personally. We may, I think,
accept Jonson's statement that he loved the man, but this side of
idolatry. The idolatry a later age would furnish.

II

But the story does not, of course, end with this handful of references. It is in the nature of traditions that they are more picturesque than facts; hence the image formed by posterity would in large
measure be fashioned by the mythos. The chief document is the
famous account of Shakespeare and Jonson in the memoir of the
former that appears in the *History of the Worthies of England*
(1662) by "the great Tom Fuller" (as Pepys termed him):

[2]See Leishman's discussion, pp. 59-60, 336n.

Many were the *wit-combates* betwixt him and *Ben Johnson*, which two I behold like a *Spanish great Gallion* and an *English Man of War*; Master *Johnson* (like the former) was built far higher in Learning; *Solid*, but *Slow* in his performances. *Shake-spear* with the *English-man of War*, lesser in *bulk*, but lighter in *sailing*, could turn with all tides, tack about and take advantage of all winds, by the quickness of his Wit and Invention.[3]

"Which two I behold," writes Fuller. The picture he has formed is clearly in his mind's eye; this is a literary evocation, not a reminiscence derived from report. The impression is confirmed by the rest of Fuller's short biography, which is starkly devoid of concrete data. Although he combed the countryside in quest of matter for his *Worthies*, he failed to learn the year of Shakespeare's death, for which he leaves a pathetic blank in his text. Yet the date is plain to see on the monument in Stratford Church.

Other sources, however, give samples of extemporaneous wit. In a mid seventeenth-century manuscript miscellany, *Merry Passages and Jests*, Sir Nicholas L'Estrange records how Jonson, after the christening of one of his infants, came upon Shakespeare, the godfather, in "a deepe study." Why so melancholy? asked Jonson. "[N]o faith *Ben*: (says he) not I, but I haue beene considering a great while what should be the fittest gift for me to bestow vpon my God-child, and I haue resolu'd at last; I pry'the what, sayes he? I faith *Ben*: I'le e'en giue him a douzen good Lattin Spoones, and thou shalt translate them."[4] (For modern readers this merry jest requires a gloss: *latten* was a brass or brass-like alloy.) The same story appears in the Plume manuscripts, but there it is Shakespeare's offspring that is being christened, and Jonson who delivers this devastating stroke of wit. Also in Plume we find Jonson beginning an epitaph: "Here lies Ben Johnson – who was once one – " and Shakespeare taking the pen from him to write:

Here lies Benjamin – with short hair upon his Chin –
Who while he lived was a slow thing – & now he's buried is no thing.[5]

An anonymous version (*c.* 1650) of the same anecdote gives it a tavern setting, but not until a century later does legend place the

---

[3]Fuller, *Worthies*, Warwick-Shire, p. 126.
[4]E. K. Chambers, *William Shakespeare: A Study of Facts and Problems* (1930), II, 243.
[5]*Ibid.*, p. 247.

two great men under a similar roof. In the *Town Jester*, around 1760, the following item appears:

Ben Johnson and Shakespeare were once at a tavern-club where there were several lords from the court who went to hear their wit and conversation; Shakespeare call'd upon Ben Johnson to give a toast; he nam'd that lord's wife that sat near him; the nobleman demanded why he nam'd her: Why not, replied the poet, she has the qualifications of a toast, being both brown and dry; which answer made them all laugh, his lordship having been obliged to marry her against his inclinations.[6]

From the notebooks of John Ward, vicar of Stratford from 1662 to 1681, we learn of the last convivial episode of Shakespeare's career and its sad aftermath. "Shakespear, Drayton, and Ben Jhonson, had a merry meeting," Ward writes, "and itt seems drank too hard, for Shakespear died of a feavour there contracted. . . ."[7] Some biographers, most recently A. L. Rowse, have attached weight to this report, and indeed Drayton, a Warwickshireman, sometimes stayed in the village of Clifford Chambers nearby to Stratford. But elsewhere Ward (who had to remind himself to peruse Shakespeare's plays in order to avoid ignorance in that matter) turns out to be no very reliable informant, for he absurdly exaggerates the dramatist's income.

None of the authorities thus far mentioned hints at sinister undercurrents of bad feeling in the relations between Jonson and Shakespeare. Not until late in the seventeenth century do we find suggested the opposing image of a malevolent Jonson, with gentle Shakespeare the innocent object of his jealousy and spite. In this connection Dryden stands at the crossroads of criticism. His attitudes towards Jonson, complex and ambivalent, might well furnish matter for another paper. We remember Dryden as expressing a high opinion of Shakespeare's rival. More than once he describes Jonson as the most judicious of poets, an English Virgil; *The Silent Woman*, examined by Dryden in the first extended critique of an Elizabethan play, he preferred before all other comedies. Yet in his own day Dryden gained a reputation as Jonson's foe, a charge he repudiated in his Preface to *An Evening's Love* (1671): *"I know I have been accus'd as an enemy of his writings; but without any other reason than that I do not admire him blindly, and*

[6]*Ibid.*, p. 286.
[7] *Ibid.*, p. 250.

without looking into his imperfections." Elsewhere, indeed, he criticizes Jonson's faults of language and wit. He describes him as "a learned plagiary." But most fraught with consequence is a brief passage in the *Discourse Concerning the Original and Progress of Satire* (1692) in which he characterizes Jonson's tribute to Shakespeare's memory as "an insolent, sparing, and invidious panegyric" – to which Jonson might have replied in precisely the words used by Dryden in his Preface to *An Evening's Love.*[8]

Dryden may also have supplied Rowe, as he did Gildon, with the story, probably apocryphal, of a memorable meeting between Jonson, Davenant, Suckling and others, at which tempers flared and Suckling warmly defended Shakespeare from Jonson's repeated slurs about want of learning and ignorance of the ancients. The episode appears in Rowe's *Account* of Shakespeare's life, the first attempt at an authoritative memoir. In the same sketch, which prefaces his 1709 edition of Shakespeare's *Works,* Rowe describes the "remarkable piece of humanity and good Nature" with which the dramatist began his acquaintance with Jonson. The latter, as yet unknown, had offered the company a play which, after a superficial perusal, they curtly refused; but Shakespeare, happening to see the script, liked it so well that he persuaded the players to reverse their decision. In this way did Jonson make his debut as a playwright. "After this they were profess'd Friends," Rowe continues,

> tho' I don't know whether the other ever made him an equal return of Gentleness and Sincerity. *Ben* was naturally Proud and Insolent, and in the Days of his Reputation did so far take upon him the Supremacy in Wit, that he could not but look with an evil Eye upon any one that seem'd to stand in Competition with him. And if at times he has affected to commend him, it has always been with some Reserve, insinuating his Uncorrectness, a careless manner of Writing, and want of Judgment. . . .[9]

This passage, paraphrasing and expanding Dryden, drops out of later editions of the *Account,* and it was popularly supposed that

[8]The extremely influential remark made in the *Discourse Concerning Satire* has received insufficient notice. Aden does not include it in his dictionary of *The Critical Opinions of John Dryden*; Chambers omits it from the Dryden references in the second volume of his *Shakespeare,* as do Herford and Simpson from the ampler body of Dryden extracts in Vol. XI of their edition of Jonson.

[9]Shakespeare, *Works,* ed. Rowe (1709), I, xiii.

the author himself had upon second thought retracted his unflattering portrayal of Jonson. But Pope, not Rowe, deserves credit – if that is the right word – for the castration. An editor who felt no compunctions about improving upon Shakespeare would hardly regard Rowe's text as sacrosanct, nor did Pope deem it necessary to draw attention to his tamperings when he reprinted the *Account* in his 1725 *Shakespeare.*

Indeed, the laureate of Twickenham took a view different from Rowe's of Shakespeare's and Jonson's relations. Anecdotal Spence records an observation made by Pope around 1728. "It was, and is, a general opinion," he remarked, "that Ben Jonson and Shakespeare lived in enmity against one another. Betterton has assured me often that there was nothing in it, and that such a supposition was founded only on the two parties which in their lifetime listed under one, and endeavoured to lessen the character of the other mutually."[10] Note that Betterton, cited by Pope as his authority, was also Rowe's informant on the facts of Shakespeare's life. Note too that, thus early, Pope refers to the *general opinion* of enmity between Jonson and Shakespeare. This tide of opinion he attempted to reverse in his own Preface. "It is an acknowledged fact," Pope asserts, "that *Ben Johnson* was introduced upon the Stage, and his first works encouraged, by *Shakespear.* [How easily does hearsay gain acceptance as fact!] And after his death, that Author writes *To the memory of his beloved Mr.* William Shakespear, which shows as if the friendship had continued thro' life. I cannot for my own part find any thing *Invidious* or *Sparing* in those verses, but wonder Mr. *Dryden* was of that opinion."[11] Pope goes on to point out the exalted status conferred upon Shakespeare by Jonson in his eulogy; also, the note of personal kindness expressed in the *Discoveries.* But despite Pope's formidable reputation, and despite his censorship of Rowe, the darker view of relations between the two dramatists persisted, and indeed gained ground.

[10]Joseph Spence, *Observations, Anecdotes, and Characters of Books and Men,* ed. James M. Osborn (1966), I, 23.
[11]Shakespeare, *Works,* ed. Pope (1725), I, xii.

III

"I cannot give into the Opinion, that *Johnson's* Friendship to *Shake-spear* continu'd through Life," John Roberts ("a Stroling Player") replied to Pope,

> or even was faithfully preserv'd any part of it, and therein beg Pardon, that once more dissent from this *infallible* EDITOR: If it is an acknowledg'd Fact that *Ben. Johnson* was introduc'd upon the Stage, and his first Works encourag'd by *Shakespear,* How mean, how base, and malevolent does it appear in him, to pick out a single Sentence from all his Writings, and misquote it after his Friend's Decease, in order to reproach him with Weakness of Judgment, and expose him to Ridcule [*sic*] and Laughter?[12]

Robert's outburst of indignation does not end with his rhetorical question; in a similarly prejudiced vein, he goes on to castigate Jonson for his "prejudic'd Pen."

On 23 April 1748 *The General Advertiser* carried a letter from an anonymous correspondent, in fact Charles Macklin the actor, on the occasion of a revival of Ford's *The Lover's Melancholy* for the benefit of Mrs. Macklin. The writer claims to have found a pamphlet entitled "Old *Ben's Light Heart* made heavy by Young *John's Melancholy Lover,*" and containing anecdotes about Jonson, Ford, and Shakespeare. The following extract will indicate the temper of Macklin's letter:

> *Ben* was by nature *splentic and sour*; with a share of envy, (for every anxious genius has some) more than was warrantable in society. By education rather *critically* than *politely* learned; which swell'd his mind into an ostentatious pride *of his own works*, and an overbearing *inexorable* judgment of his *contemporaries.*
>
> This raised him many enemies, who towards the close of his life endeavoured to dethrone *this tyrant*, as the pamphlet stiles him, out of the dominion of the theatre. And what greatly contributed to their design, was the *slights* and *malignances* which the *rigid Ben* too frequently threw out against the *lowly Shakspeare*, whose fame since his death, as appears by the pamphlet, was grown too great for *Ben's envy* either to *bear* with or *wound.*
>
> It would greatly exceed the limits of your paper to set down all the *contempts* and *invectives* which were uttered and written by

[12][John Roberts], *An Answer to Mr. Pope's Preface to Shakespear* (1729), pp. 10-11.

Ben, and are collected and produced in *this pamphlet,* as unanswerable and shaming evidences to prove his *ill-nature* and *ingratitude* to *Shakspeare,* who first introduced him to the *theatre and fame.*[13]

Macklin's solicitude for an editor pressed for space does not prevent him from including a few choice samples of Ben's contempts and invectives. These, being old hat, cannot be said to swell the record, and anyway the rare pamphlet turns out to be a creature of Macklin's own imagination, invented to puff a revival from which he had expectations of pecuniary gain. So much Edmond Malone demonstrates in an essay that reads like a dry run for his celebrated unmasking of the more sensational impostures of William Henry Ireland.

The Macklin forgery is symptomatic of a curious state of literary affairs. With the decline of Jonson's reputation and the concurrent rise of bardolatry, the poet formerly preferred to Shakespeare by the intelligentsia became a favourite target for denigration. One sees the process at work in the article on Jonson in that popular compendium, the *Biographia Britannica* (1750). The anonymous memorialist is not sparing of those slights and malignances for which Jonson was being taken to task. Ben's chosen spelling of his surname is cited as "one instance, among innumerable others, of that affectation, which so strongly marks the character of our poet." Elsewhere in the same piece we hear of his "hardy and sullen" temper, and of the "presumption and vanity" of the *Ode to Himself.* His natural disposition, we are told, was no more respectable than his corpulent and bulky physique, his hard and rocky countenance; Drummond's unflattering impressions of his guest receive prominent display. The author does not dwell upon Jonson's relations with Shakespeare, but his characterization of the latter as "that humane good-natured bard" implies a contrast between the two men which had already become a biographical commonplace.

The contrast is magnified by the commentators. Farmer is an exception; in his *Essay on the Learning of Shakespeare* (1767) he describes Jonson's eulogy as "the warmest Panegyrick that ever was written," and concludes, "In truth the received opinion of the pride and malignity of Jonson, at least in the earlier part of his life, is absolutely groundless." (Note, however, the phrase "received opinion.") The others of this generation – Chalmers, Steevens, Malone

[13]The letter is reproduced by Malone (Shakespeare, *Plays and Poems* [1790], Vol. I, Pt. i, 203), from whose text I quote.

– who deserve all honour for their contributions to our knowledge
of Shakespeare, appear in a less flattering light when it comes to
Jonson. They scrutinized his text with all the critical instruments at
their disposal, and found imagined sneers where previously none
had been suspected.

In his *Supplemental Apology* (1799), Chalmers is the first to
identify the Bard as Jonson's target in his fifty-sixth epigram:

> Poor Poet-Ape, that would be thought our chief,
>> Whose works are e'en the frippery of wit,
> From brokage is become so bold a thief,
>> As we, the robb'd, leave rage, and pity it.
> At first, he made low shifts, would pick, and glean;
>> By the reversion of old plays, now grown
> Into a little wealth, and credit in the scene,
>> He takes up all, makes each man's wit his own. . . .[14]

There is nothing in these lines to suggest that Shakespeare is their
object, apart from the presumption that he *must* be the victim of
any attack directed by Jonson against any unspecified poet. Chalmers' *aperçu* perhaps does not come unexpectedly from a critic
who has the distinction of being the first to propose that the Fair
Youth of Shakespeare's sonnets is the ageing Queen Elizabeth. His
discussion of the Poet-Ape later threw Jonson's editor Gifford into
one of those fits of apoplexy to which the imbecilities of commentators made him prone. "Mr. Chalmers," he explodes, "will *take it on
his death* that the person here meant is Shakspeare! Who can doubt
it? For my part, I am persuaded, that GROOM IDIOT in the next epigram is also Shakspeare; and, indeed, generally, that he is typified
by the words 'fool and knave,' so exquisitely descriptive of him,
wherever they occur in Jonson."[15]

The terrible scene in *Lear* of the blinding of Gloucester, and its
aftermath of the servant going to fetch flax and egg whites to apply
to the bleeding face, has evoked extraordinary responses from
critics. An eminent psychoanalyst has suggested that the blood and
bandage represent the surfacing of the poet's suppressed childhood
memories of his mother's menstruation. The gloss offered by Shakespeare's eighteenth-century editor Steevens, while less sublime,
deserves to be regarded with equal solemnity. He finds Jonson

[14]See Chalmers, *Supplemental Apology*, pp. 235-42.
[15]Jonson, *Works*, ed. Gifford (1816), VIII, 181, n.4.

expressing his scorn for *Lear* in Act II, scene vii, of *The Case Is Altered*, dated 1609 by Steevens. Here Juniper urges Martino, whose head has been broken in a fencing match, to "go, get a white of an egge, and a little flax, and close the breach of the head, it is the most conducible thing that can be." Steevens forgets to mention that flax and egg whites must have been a common Elizabethan remedy for such injuries; nor does he say that 1609 is the publication date for *The Case Is Altered*, not the year of first performance, which took place almost a decade before *Lear*. Malone exposed Steevens' error but, unwilling to part with a good thing, suggested that Jonson had interpolated his dig between the appearance of Shakespeare's play and the printing of his own.

In truth Malone, greatest of Shakespeare's eighteenth-century editors, did more than anyone up to his time to advance the myth of personal enmity between his idol and Jonson. Again and again in his notes he harps upon Jonson's clumsy sarcasms and malevolent reflections. "In the *Silent Woman*, 1609, Jonson perhaps pointed at Shakspeare as one whom he viewed with *scornful* yet *jealous* eyes...." "In the *Devil's an Ass*, all Shakspeare's *historical plays* are obliquely *censured*." "The Induction to the *Staple of News*, 1625, contains a *sneer* at *Julius Caesar*." And so on; many more instances might be adduced. In his reprint of Rowe's *Account* for his 1790 *Shakspeare*, Malone resurrects in a note the passage (already mentioned) excised by Pope, and he goes on to describe Jonson's "envious disposition" as "notorious" in his own day, and to picture Ben as "pouring out against those who preferred our poet to him, a torrent of illiberal abuse."[16] Coming from so eminent an authority, Malone's illiberal abuse of Jonson carried weight. Currency too, for Rowe's *Account* with Malone's notes would be more than once reprinted.

IV

Eventually a reaction came to eighteenth-century Jonson-baiting, and this shift in the critical wind I would attribute to the new-found interest in Shakespeare's contemporaries as dramatists fascinating in their own right, and not as lesser breeds useful merely to illustrate obscure phrases of the Immortal Bard. Jonson found his first notable defender in Octavius Gilchrist, who brought out

[16]Shakespeare, *Plays and Poems*, ed. Malone, Vol. I, Pt. i, pp. 111-13, n.3.

S. Schoenbaum

An Examination of the Charges Maintained by Messrs. Malone
Chalmers, and Others, of Ben Jonson's Enmity, &c. towards Shake
speare in 1808, significantly the same year that witnessed the pub
lication of Lamb's *Specimens*, which marked a new tide in the
affairs of poets. If Jonson was indeed the ungrateful libeller of his
friend, Gilchrist declares, "his writings ought to be condemned to
the hands of the hangman, and his name be consigned to perpetual
infamy." (But why, even if Jonson were a cad, for that reason throw
out *Volpone* and *The Alchemist*? This is the very ecstasy of
bardolatry.)

> If, however, [Gilchrist continues] it shall appear that his fair fam
> has been blackened, his memory traduced, and his writings per
> verted, for the unworthy purpose of raising a rival poet on the ruin
> of his reputation; and that malevolent critics may display thei
> sagacity and accuteness in tracing passages applicable to thei
> favourite poet; the voice of public justice, it is to be hoped, wil
> restore to the brow of the poet his violated honours, committing to
> merited shame and obloquy the "viperous" critics by whom they
> were bereaved.[17]

Clearly Jonson had found an eloquent champion. Gilchrist pro
ceeds to sift "the ample dunghill of antiquarian defamation," point
ing out the excesses of Steevens, Malone, and Chalmers. He make
short work of the Macklin forgery and of the Poet-Ape; but exces
breeds excess. In acquitting his hero of imputed girds at Shake
speare, he goes so far as to deny allusions where they indubitably
exist, as in the Prologue to *Every Man in His Humour* and the
Induction to *Bartholomew Fair*: Jonson's satire must always be
general, and never have personal application. A similar whitewash
ing occurs when Gilchrist cites Jonson's passage on Shakespeare in
Discoveries – he quotes only the favourable bits, passing over in
silence honest Ben's censure of his friend's supposed lapses. An
edition of Ford by Weber in 1811, reviving the discredited Macklin
pamphlet and charges of "the bitterness of Ben Johnson against his
too powerful rival," moved Gilchrist to buckle on his armour again
in *A Letter to William Gifford, Esq.* (1811). But it is the latter who
now moves to the centre of the stage as Jonson's most impassioned
defender.

Urbanity is not Gifford's forte, as it is Gilchrist's, but he make
up for this deficiency by the vigour of his prejudiced polemics in

[17]Gilchrist, *Examination*, pp. 6-7.

14

is edition of Jonson's *Works* (1816). Generously acknowledging is friend's pioneering contribution, Gifford devotes a whole sec- on to rebuttal of "Proofs of Ben Jonson's Malignity, from the Commentators on Shakspeare." The introductory memoir contains nany curious declarations. Gifford would have us believe that in 598 "Jonson was as well known as Shakspeare, and perhaps, bet- er" (so much for Meres!). He dismisses *Pericles* as "worthless." He dmits to surreptitious expurgation of the text: "I know the impor- ance of fidelity; but no considerations on earth can tempt me to ne wanton or heedless propagation of impiety." (Editors please ote.) But Gifford's chief contribution is to envisage, so far as I now for the first time in print, Shakespeare's participation in the appy sessions of the wits at the Mermaid Tavern:

> Sir Walter Raleigh . . . had instituted a meeting of *beaux esprits* at the Mermaid, a celebrated tavern in Friday-street, of this club, which combined more talent and genius, perhaps, than ever met before or since, our author was a member; and here, for many years, he regularly repaired with Shakspeare, Beaumont, Fletcher, Selden, Cotton, Carew, Martin, Donne, and many others, whose names, even at this distant period, call up a mingled feeling of reverence and respect. Here, in the full flow and confidence of friendship, the lively and interesting "wit-combats" took place between Shakspeare and our author; and hither, in probable allu- sion to them, Beaumont fondly lets his thoughts wander, in his letter to Jonson, from the country.
> ———"What things have we seen,
> Done at the MERMAID! . . ."[18]

t is strange to find the haughty Raleigh presiding over tavern igh-jinks attended by Shakespeare – especially when one consid- rs that from the accession of James until after the poet's death the night was imprisoned in the Tower. Nor, despite the fact that hakespeare knew the landlord of the Mermaid (as is attested by a eal-estate transaction of 1613), is there any evidence that he was a nember of any club that met at this tavern or anywhere else. The essions at the Mermaid conjured up by Gifford belong not to ne historical record but to a nineteenth-century critic's romantic ancy; so I. A. Shapiro has conclusively shown in an important rticle.[19] In the pages of Gifford's *Jonson* we witness the birth of a

---

[18]Jonson, *Works*, ed. Gifford, I, lxv-lxvi.
[19]"The 'Mermaid Club'," *MLR*, XLV (1950), 6-17.

legend, although one for which hints had been supplied by Fulle
and traditionary anecdotes.

Artists would sketch Shakespeare and Jonson and the other wit
with meticulous Victorian verisimilitude. Poets would furnish th
scene with words. In George Willis Cooke's *Guide-book to th
Poetic and Dramatic Works of Robert Browning* (1891), I find th
following commentary on "At the 'Mermaid' ": "In this poem th
speaker is Shakespeare, to whom it has just been suggested that h
is to be the next great poet. He is speaking to his literary friend
especially to Ben Jonson, gathered at 'The Mermaid' tavern, th
favorite resort in London of the Elizabethan wits."[20] A scholar
sentimental romance has been canonized as fact. Inevitably th
supposed fact would be fictionalized as romance. There is a del
cious scene in a light modern novel in which Shakespeare, Jonson
Raleigh, Sidney, and other worthies are assembled at the Mermaid
Through the open window float the voices of prentice lads singin
"Drink to me only with thine eyes. . . ." "O rare Ben Jonson
exclaims the Bard, weeping, as the voices die away. "God," Jonso
nods sadly, "what genius I had then!"[21]

V

The next important development occurs later in the century, wit
the emergence of a rage for topical allusions, particularly as the
were to be found in plays purportedly connected with the so-calle
War of the Theatres. In *Shakespeare and Jonson, Dramatic verse
Wit Combats* (1864), Robert Cartwright proposed that in *Ever
Man in His Humour* Shakespeare is represented by both the tow
sophisticate Wellbred and the country gull Stephen; moreover, i
Poetaster "there can be little doubt" that Ovid stands for the Bard
Cartwright makes many other ingenious suggestions: Shakespear
replied to *Every Man out of His Humour* in *Much Ado*. He vente
his wrath upon Jonson in the character of Apemantus in *Timon
And "Who can doubt that Iago is malignant Ben?" asks Cartwrigh
and does not stay for an answer. An anonymous critic, probabl
Simpson, in *The North British Review* (1870), identified Amorphu
(the Deformed) in *Cynthia's Revels* as Shakespeare who, we lear
with some surprise, had been nicknamed "Deformed" because of h

[20]Pp. 41-42.
[21]Caryl Brahms and S. J. Simon, *No Bed for Bacon* (1941), pp. 133-34.

ignorance and plagiarisms. This is crazy stuff, and there is a lot more of it. But the Rev. Frederick Gard Fleay is someone to be taken more seriously.

In 1874 the eccentric headmaster of Skipton Grammar School took the just established New Shakspere Society by storm with a series of papers on chronology and authorship. Fleay is the first of the great modern disintegrators of Shakespeare's text. As he proceeded from instalment to instalment his views became increasingly bizarre, until they proved too much for the Society which had provided him with a forum. Turning from statistical studies, for which he was not especially well suited by reason of his inability to add, Fleay compiled annals of the stage and ferreted out topical references which, to his delight, appeared everywhere.

Only the Jonson-Shakespeare allusions here concern us. About *Twelfth Night* Fleay writes in his *Life of Shakespeare* (1886): "I believe that Sir Toby represents Jonson and Malvolio Marston; but that subject requires to be treated in a separate work from its complexity."[22] This monograph, alas, never appeared, although Fleay elsewhere elaborated somewhat his comment on *Twelfth Night*. He identifies *Troilus and Cressida* as the purge which, according to *The Return from Parnassus*, Shakespeare administered to Jonson, "Ajax representing Jonson, Achilles Chapman, and Hector Shakespeare." In his *Biographical Chronicle of the English Drama* (1891), he enlarges on this hypothesis:

> . . . whoever will take the trouble to compare the description of Crites in *Cynthia's Revels*, ii.1, with that of Ajax in *Troylus and Cressida*, i.2, will see that Ajax is Jonson: slow as the Elephant, crowded by Nature with "humors," valiant as the Lion, churlish as the Bear, melancholy without cause (compare Macilente). Hardly a word is spoken of or by Ajax in ii.3, iii.3, which does not apply literally to Jonson; and in ii.1 he beats Thersites of the "mastic jaws," i.3, 73 (Histriomastix, Theriomastix), as Jonson "beat Marston," *Drum. Conv.*, 11.[23]

And how did the unknown Cambridge playwright find out that Shakespeare had administered a purge to Jonson in a play never clapper-clawed by the palms of the vulgar? He saw it in production when the Chamberlain's Men visited the university in 1601. Q.E.D.

Fleay's work, highly influential in its own day, left a mark on

[22]*A Chronicle History of the Life and Work of William Shakespeare*, p. 220.
[23]I, 366.

Josiah H. Penniman's *The War of the Theatres* (1897), and also on Roscoe Addison Small's *The Stage Quarrel Between Ben Jonson and the So-called Poetasters* (1899), which however is more critical. Still, Small can say that "No Elizabethan audience could hear Alexander's description of Ajax [*Troilus and Cressida*, I, ii] without at once thinking of Jonson."[24] This just goes to show, I suppose, the advantage that an Elizabethan audience had over a modern one.

What inferences are we to draw from this selective and no doubt superficial survey? My last remark, about Penniman and Small, may serve to illustrate the hold that the past has upon the present: these mouldy dissertations, seventy years old, must still be cited as the latest authorities on the War of the Theatres, and Shakespeare's and Jonson's roles therein.[25] But our scholarly inheritance is everywhere about us. A presumed sneer at Shakespeare in *Every Man out of His Humour*, first detected by Steevens in the eighteenth century and effectively countered by Gifford in 1816, has in recent years been exhumed. A gifted researcher like Leslie Hotson can blandly assume the existence of a Mermaid Club with a membership including Shakespeare and other *beaux esprits*. Despite Gilchrist and Gifford there are twentieth-century students who insist that Shakespeare is Jonson's Poet-Ape, and that old Ben felt evil in his heart towards benevolent Will.[26]

Old ghosts, then, haunt biography and criticism. It has been my purpose in this paper to exorcise a few of them, and to help restore the picture, overlaid with the dust of centuries, of two excellent playwrights who sometimes laboured for the same company, and who took a lively interest in one another's work: Shakespeare by acting in *Every Man in His Humour* and in *Sejanus*, Jonson by his scattered remarks, not always approving, on his great colleague's writings. How intimate were the terms of their relationship, what tensions (if any) underlay the surface, we cannot at this remove of time ascertain. But we may rest assured that Heminge and Condell

---

[24]P. 169.

[25]Re-evaluation is, however, at last underway; since this paper was written, Stuart B. Omans has completed a Northwestern University dissertation, "The War of the Theatres: An Approach to Its Origins, Development, and Meaning."

[26]Inimitably misinformed, Colin Wilson has recently remarked, in the fictional context of *The Philosopher's Stone* (1969), "Jonson referred to Shakespeare as a 'Poet-ape' in *The Return from Parnassus*."

would not have invited Jonson to contribute the principal eulogy of the First Folio if he were not their fellow's friend, and Jonson would not have penned so noble a tribute if he did not esteem Shakespeare as an artist and treasure him as a comrade. Nor would he have, in the privacy of his study, described Shakespeare with a warmth that he expressed for no other poet. We may believe that he loved the man; to be sure, on this side idolatry. That is not an unpleasant note on which to end.

The Children of Paul's, 1551-1582

TREVOR LENNAM

It is not possible to say when Master Sebastian Westcott first presented boys in stage plays; his collegiate or, perhaps, monastic experience in Devon may well have fitted him to train, supervise and educate choristers long before we find him at Court in 1545. There is little doubt, however, that by the time Westcott was a Vicar Choral in 1547 he had become acquainted with the circle of writers and musicians associated with John Redford and John Heywood at St. Paul's, and involved with the dramatic work of the two men. Redford was then nearing the end of his life and Westcott was soon to succeed him as Almoner and Master of the Choristers. Heywood, at fifty years of age, possibly no longer a singer of distinction and very likely no longer writing plays, was nevertheless still active as an instrumentalist, epigrammatist, poet and court entertainer. His association with Redford's choristers may have begun as early as 1537-8 when he presented an interlude "with his children" before the Princess Mary.[1] He continued to associate himself (in what precise way it is not clear) with the stage presentations by Paul's boys in 1551-2 and in 1559. He was also a prominent contributor to the miscellany of music, verse and fragments of Redford's plays, apparently an uncompleted collection of the work of a St. Paul's literary and musical circle very possibly gathered together after the death of Redford.[2] Westcott's connection with

[1] For evidence of Heywood's connection with Redford and Westcott see Arthur Brown, "Two Notes on John Redford," *MLR*, XLIII (Oct., 1948), 508-10.
[2] BM MS, Add. 15233. The other contributors from St. Paul's were: Thomas Prideaux, John Thorne, Myles Huggard and Master Knight. See Arthur Brown's brief description of the MS in *Grove's Dictionary of Music and Musicians*, fifth edition (London, 1954), VII, 79-81.

this volume is *sub silentio*. In addition to his association with Redford and Heywood, he was on friendly terms with at least two other contributors, Thomas Prideaux and John Thorne. *The Marriage of Wit and Science*, very probably presented at court by Westcott in 1567-8, and recorded in the *Revels Accounts* as "witte and will," was an adaptation of Redford's *Wit and Science*, a very substantial portion of which is in the manuscript. Finally, there is A. W. Reed's plausible suggestion that the "booke of ditties written," given by Westcott to Queen Mary on New Year's Day, 1557, may have been based upon the manuscript repertory of St. Paul's songs.[3]

During the short reigns of Edward and of Mary the Paul's boys were not in demand, and records of their appearances in plays at court are as meagre as they are uncertain. Most of the performances before Edward were either given by the Chapel or by the King's Players. As soon as Mary came to the throne, she prohibited performances of interludes and plays without royal licence, fearing the controversy that might result from matters touching religious doctrine.[4] She was not occasionally averse to witnessing an approved play at court, but on the whole seems to have preferred masques and pastimes and, of course, musical entertainment for which she had a special aptitude and liking. Unlike Elizabeth, neither of these sovereigns was particularly impressed by the appeal of the children's companies. However, the Paul's boys found themselves welcome elsewhere. They were invited to entertain the Guild of Merchant Taylors on St. John's Day in 1549, 1551 and again in 1554. On all these occasions the choristers were paid for playing upon viols and singing, and upon the last visit they shared the program with the musicians of "my Lord of Pembroke."[5]

Westcott's boys played before the eighteen-year-old Princess Elizabeth at Hatfield House in 1551-2, and on that occasion Heywood was in attendance either as entrepreneur or as a musician. This is the only unquestionable record of a performance by Paul's boys before Elizabeth earlier than her coronation. In view of her immediate preference for Westcott's company after her accession,

[3]*Early Tudor Drama* (London, 1926), p. 58.
[4]Proclamation dated 16 August, 1553, printed by J. P. Collier, *The History of English Dramatic Poetry* (3 vols., London, 1831), I, 157-58.
[5]See C. M. Clode, *Memorials of the Guild of Merchant Taylors* (London, 1875), p. 526 and pp. 528-29. Perhaps this association with the Merchant Taylors was encouraged, if not inspired, by Sir Thomas White who employed Sebastian's brother, Philip.

one suspects that her delight in them was founded upon a more substantial acquaintance than that merely afforded by a single presentation, however memorable. We may be inclined, therefore, to give some credence to the not unlikely possibility of a Paul's performance at Hatfield House in either 1554 or 1557.

Elizabeth's notable predilection for the children's companies and, above all, for Westcott's boys has remained something of a mystery. Hillebrand suggests that Westcott "was *persona grata* for being an old friend of Elizabeth's," but goes on to admit that it "hardly enables us to understand why Westcott's company was so much more acceptable than the Chapel or indeed, we might add, than any other company."[6] Sir Edmund Chambers discussed the problem in the light of the renaissance humanistic tradition and pointed out the long history of the Chapel entertainers, "the decay of the royal interluders" and the fact that the "other professional companies had not yet found an economic basis in London."[7] To these explanations another may be added. After Elizabeth's accession the boys of cathedral and chapel were no longer so busily engaged in the performance of duties, ceremonies and rituals associated with the old faith. The reformed religious services must have increased the freedom of the choristers from daily ecclesiastical duties. This is very likely the reason why the Paul's boys did not, so far as we know, appear in plays before the devout Mary during her reign, when the cathedral once more resumed its central place in the religious and civic life of London.[8]

Hillebrand's suggestion that Westcott enjoyed the special favour of Elizabeth because he was an old friend would certainly seem true by, say, 1570; there is little doubt that she indirectly but effectively protected him from clerical authority in the early sixties, and also that, although often capricious, she was unswervingly faithful to old friends. It does not, however, explain her patronage of his company at the very beginning of her reign; the records of only one, perhaps two, presentations by him before the young Princess are all we possess as evidence of their acquaintance. In pursuing the answer to this puzzling question, it is perhaps more fruitful to

[6]*The Child Actors* (New York, 1964), p. 74.
[7]*Elizabethan Stage* (Oxford, 1923), II, 4.
[8]It is significant that the only visit the Paul's choristers made to her court was in a ceremony of the Boy Bishop in 1554.

glance at Elizabeth's preference for the "quality" of the Paul's boys, rather than at her patronage of her servant, Sebastian. The most important clue to this preference lies in the Queen's temperament. Throughout her life she rarely failed to respond to the appeal of intelligent and accomplished youth, particularly to handsome, audacious and eloquent boys. Wherever she went the grace and ingenuousness of young men and boys charmed her and drew from her praise, if not reward. Westcott's enduring success in pleasing the Queen was based, perhaps not altogether without conscious intent, upon an appeal to this deeply-rooted susceptibility within Elizabeth – the product of the conditioning factors of her early life and of her later circumstances.[9] After all, many others traded upon this partiality in other ways and to much greater profit than the Almoner of St. Paul's.

Two records early in the reign show that Westcott recognized and was willing to grasp the opportunity of consolidating his initial enterprise as a court entertainer. The first promotion, whether occurring fortuitously or achieved by foresight, gave him a new measure of freedom. Arthur Brown has drawn attention to the implications of the wording of Sebastian's re-appointment as Almoner on December 1, 1559: "Previously Westcott was to exercise his office 'in persona sua propria.' Now he may exercise it 'per se vel sufficientem deputatem suam sive deputatos suos sufficientes.' " Brown has observed that the appointment of a deputy or deputies would give the Almoner more time for his dramatic activities, and also would permit him to be absent from St. Paul's.[10] The second record explains the use Westcott was to make of this contingency. Seven months later he was empowered by a royal warrant to "take-up" boys from other collegiate and cathedral churches "within our Reallme" for service at St. Paul's, and ecclesiastical authorities were advised to co-operate "whereof ffail ye nott as ye tender our favour

<hr>

[9]See Elizabeth Jenkins, *Elizabeth the Great* (London, 1958), for one of the most perceptive studies of "That long-preserved virginity," in which many instances of Elizabeth's delighted response to bright youngsters are recorded.
[10]"Three Notes on Sebastian Westcott," *MLR*, XLIV (April, 1949), 230, and "Sebastian Westcott at York," *MLR*, XLVII (Jan., 1952), 49-50. Were Gyles Clothier and John Boult, the musician, who were beneficiaries of Westcott's will, and who were mentioned immediately after the bequest to the "tenne choristers" and in the middle of a list of bequests to cathedral officials, Sebastian Westcott's deputy almoners in 1582?

and will answere for the contrary."[11] Westcott's commission is similar to the one granted to St. George's Chapel on March 8, 1560, and shows that the Queen intended to have not only excellent choral establishments at Windsor and at St. Paul's but also worthy acting companies, since the boys taken up for service "would be chosen as much for their histrionic as for their singing ability."[12] In the spring of 1571 Westcott visited York in search of singing boys, and since his commission was transcribed in the Minute Book of the City, he may have succeeded in persuading John Thorne, the cathedral organist, to part with a promising lad.[13] It would appear that Sebastian's customary search for new boys was made not long after the festive season at court ended. In the spring of 1580 he took up a boy from Christ's Hospital.[14]

By 1560 Sebastian Westcott was well prepared for future service to the Queen. As successor to John Redford he had gained considerable experience at St. Paul's since 1547; he had also inherited Redford's repertory of plays. He was already familiar with the Queen's theatrical taste as a result of several successful presentations, at least two of them in association with the elderly and very experienced musician and dramatist, John Heywood. He had lately acquired extended power as Almoner and Master of the Choristers for the improvement of his company. Ahead of him lay over twenty years of almost uninterrupted dramatic presentation.

Fortunately the names of many of Westcott's boys have been preserved. A comparison of the lists in which their names appear is instructive.

---

[11]Minutes of the City Council of York, 24, fol. 241, first printed in *York Civic Records*, VII, Yorkshire Archeological Society, Record Series, 125, (1950), and reprinted by Arthur Brown, *MLR*, XLVII (Jan., 1952), 49-50. The warrant is dated "the last of June in the second yere of our Reigne" and appears to have been copied into the Minute Book in May, 1571.

[12]Brown, *ibid.*, p. 50. The chief difference between the Windsor and the St. Paul's commissions is that the former was expressly forbidden to take men and boys from either the Chapel Royal or St. Paul's (see Chambers, II, 62), whereas Westcott was left quite unrestricted.

[13]Friendly co-operation from Thorne would seem likely, if he were the same Thorne whose compositions appear with Redford's and Heywood's in BM MS. Add. 15233, and with Redford's in MS. Add. 29996.

[14]"Mr. Sebastian of Paulls is appointed to have Hallawaie the younger out of this House to be one of the singing children of the Cathedral Church of Paulls in this Citie" (Court Minute 5, March, 1579-80), cited by "Dotted Chrochet," "The Children of St. Paul's and the Plays They Acted," *The Musical Times*, 1 Jan., 1907.

1554[15]	*1561*[16]	*1574*[17]
John Burde	[John Halcocke]	George Bowring
Simon Burde	[Richard Prince]	Thomas Morley
Richard Hewse	John Rainoldes	Peter Phillipp
George More	Anthony Pickeringe	Henry Nation
John Alkok	William Foxe	Robert Knight
Gilbert Maxsey	Richard Priddam	Thomas Brande
Roger Stakhouse	Samuel Bushe	Edward Pattmie
Richard Prynce	Richard/Robert Boker	Robert Baker
John Farmer	Thomas Wilkingson	Thomas Johnson
Robert Chofe	John Marshall	
	John Whalye	

1580[18]

Hallawaie the younger

Presumably Halcock (or Alcock) and Prince, who were in the choir in 1554, had by 1561 recently departed. It is possible that the Robert Boker of 1561-2 was the Robert Baker of 1574, but in view of the time span perhaps not very likely. To these names may be added those ex-choristers mentioned in Westcott's will.

Peter Phillipps and (possibly) Thomos Venge

Bromeham
Richard Huse
Robert Knight
Nicholas Carleton   "sometymes children of the
Bayle   saide Almenry howse"
Henry[?] Nasion
Gregorye Bowringe

Whether or not the Thomas Morley in the 1574 list was the great

[15]Given by Hillebrand, p. 110, from a suit in the Court of Exchequer. The John Farmer in the list may very well be the composer and instrumentalist, see *Grove's Dictionary*, III, 30-31.
[16]From Bishop Grindal's Visitation, Guildhall Library, MS. 9537/2, fols. 4-19. There are two lists: the first (April, 1561) on fol. 7 contains the names of Halcock and Prince at the head crossed through, and Boker's first name is given as Richard; the second (November, 1562) on fol. 19 omits Halcock and Prince and includes Robert Boker.
[17]Given by Hillebrand, p.111, from Bishop Sandys' Visitation, Guildhall Library, MS. 9537/3, fols. 1-5. Robert Knight in the list may possibly be the musician, see *Grove's Dictionary*, IV, 780.
[18]See n.14, p. 24.

composer is still uncertain.[19] Peter Phillips in the 1574 and 1582 lists has been identified as the recusant composer and organist.[20] He was living with Westcott in 1582 and, after his master's death, went abroad.[21] He might well have been Sebastian's assistant music master after leaving the choir. Nicholas Carleton, like John Farmer, was a later composer of vocal and instrumental music.[22] Of no renown but of great interest to us are Bowring, Nasion and Knight in the 1582 list, and Richard Hughes in the earliest one, since these persons were, like Phillips, living with Westcott in 1582, not, one supposes, in the almonry house, but quite possibly in the Sermon Lane property which was originally left to the cathedral for the express purpose of maintaining senior choristers after they had left the choir. Hughes, if indeed he is the "Hewse" of the first list, must have been about thirty years of age at the time of Westcott's death; the others may have been between sixteen and twenty-one years of age. Why was Westcott harbouring these seven former choristers? Could the answer be that they were still useful to his theatrical enterprise, perhaps aiding, and some of them even augmenting, the ten choristers in the more spectacular and demanding presentations of classical legend and history which were a prominent feature of the Paul's repertory from 1571 onwards? The number of performers in the court plays may perhaps be estimated by the numbers of pairs of gloves the Revels Office supplied to the various companies, both men's and boys'. There is a marked increase in the quantity given to the Paul's boys.[23] They were issued with a dozen pairs for *Titus and Gesippus* in 1577, and eighteen pairs for their respective presentations of *Scipio Africanus* in 1580 and of *Pompey* in 1581.[24]

[19]*DNB*, XIV, 981-82, claims the identification; *Grove's Dictionary*, V, 895-98, makes no mention of Morley's possible association with the St. Paul's choir. The composer was organist at the cathedral for a brief period in 1591.

[20]See *Grove's Dictionary*, VI, 712-15.

[21]"I geve to Peter Phillipe likewise remayning withe me sixe poundes thirtene shillinges and fower pence"; see also A. C. Petti, "Peter Phillips, Composer and Organist, 1561-1628," *Recusant History* (Bognor Regis, 1957-8), IV, 45-60.

[22]See *Grove's Dictionary*, II, 74, and also Gustave Reese, *Music in the Renaissance* (London, 1954), p. 855.

[23]The plays performed by the schools, Eton, Merchant Taylors and Westminster, invariably required more gloves than those of the chorister companies in the late sixties and early seventies. It may be that their greater resources of personnel and their more ambitious plays forced the choristers to compete with presentations of greater scope by the mid-seventies.

[24]See Albert Feuillerat, *Documents Relating to the Office of the Revels in the Time of Elizabeth* (Louvain, 1908), fols. 276, 321 and 336.

Glancing over the list of choir boys in 1574, we are reminded that one of them "being one of his principall plaiers" was abducted from Westcott's ménage in December 1575. This affair became a matter for immediate Privy Council action and a letter was sent to the Master of the Rolls and to one of the Masters of Requests instructing them to "examine such persons as Sebastian holdeth suspected and to proceade with such as be founde faultie according to Lawe...."[25] It is not known if Westcott recovered his boy; however, the loss of a star must have been a serious inconvenience, coming as it did shortly before his appointment to present a play at court.

Among the exciting and arduous undertakings the choristers were called upon to endure, once they were established as regular visitors to court, were the journeys by cart and barge to the royal palaces at Richmond, Whitehall, Greenwich and Hampton Court. Earlier in their history there were dusty perambulations to such places as Hatfield House in Hertfordshire and Nonsuch in Surrey. Later there were miserable midwinter journeys by river and one wonders at the resilience of the boys, since they gave their performances on the same night. The serpentine trip to Hampton Court was certainly the most tedious and perhaps the least to their liking. All arrangements for travel were made by the officers of the Queen's Revels, at first from Blackfriars, and, after 1560, from their accommodation at St. John's Hospital, Clerkenwell. The Paul's party – the boys, the attendant tirewoman and dressers, the stage assistants and the master – gathered at Blackfriar's wharf and boarded a wherry loaded with their playing stuff, usually returning in the early hours of the following morning.

One wonders how the choristers felt about their master. No commendatory statement about Westcott, such as Thomas Tusser's affectionate appraisal of John Redford, exists to show how he treated the fifty or so boys who must have passed through his hands during his long career. From the evidence of Westcott's bounty to the choristers in his will, domestic life in the almonry appears to have been comfortable. That he must have been as kindly regarded as his predecessor is to some extent borne out by the fact that some of his former boys remained with him after their service in the choir had ended. Certainly, to the officials at court and cathedral, to the clerks in the Revels Office and to the city

25J. R. Dasent, *Acts of the Privy Council* (London, 1890-1907), IX, 156. Hillebrand, citing *Privy Council Registers, Elizabeth*, II, 408, prints the document in full (p. 124).

authorities, he seems to have been regarded as something of a "character" by the early sixties. Thereafter, and until his death most of them referred to him as "Master Sebastian."

The earliest surviving record of the existence of Westcott's play house belongs to the end of 1575, when the Court of Aldermen were "enformed that one Sebastian that will not comvnycate with the Church of England kepe the playes and resorte of the people to great gaine and peryll of the Corruptinge of the Chyldren with papistrie," and instructed the Remembrancer to ask Dean Nowel to remedy the situation "within his iurysdyccion, as he shall see meete for Christian Relygion and good order." It is safe to infer from this that Westcott's playhouse, whether located within the walls of the churchyard or in some cathedral property just outside was, in fact, immune from civic ordinance and that it was operating successfully, drawing crowds and making a profit. Sebastian's enterprise may have started a few years earlier; indeed, it is quite possible that small audiences had watched the final rehearsals of plays commissioned for the Queen's entertainment for over a dec ade or more before his "exercise" of plays became the kind of fully fledged commercial venture which so disturbed the aldermen in 1575.[26] Nothing seems to have come from this protest; in December 1578 the Privy Council required the Lord Mayor to suffer six com panies, among them the children of Paul's, "to exercise playeng within the Cittie."[27] The only other reference to the Paul's play house made in Westcott's lifetime was Stephen Gosson's brief allusion to it in *Playes confuted in five actions* (1582).

The precise location of the Paul's playhouse remains obscure Among the places within the precinct so far proposed, we need to consider the almonry house, the hall of the college of Minor Canons, St. Gregory's Church and the Chapter or Convocation

---

[26]In the court order aldermanic indignation is directed expressly against West-cott's contumacy; however, it follows immediately after an instruction to the governors of Christ's Hospital to collect "all suche somez of monye as by an Acte of Common Counsell lately made" from Innkeepers and householders on whose premises interludes or plays took place. Perhaps the aldermen were equally upset that Westcott's "great gaine" was exempt from the dues they felt should have been surrendered by him to the sick and poor, as laid down in their Act of 6 December, 1574 (see Chambers, IV, 273-76).
[27]For Privy Council Minutes see Chambers, IV, 278.

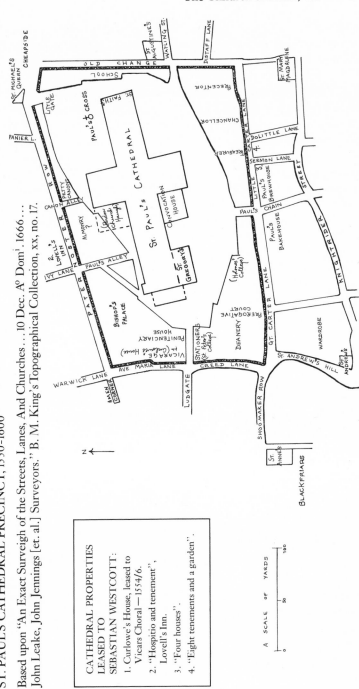

ST. PAUL'S CATHEDRAL PRECINCT, 1550-1600

Based upon "An Exact Surveigh of the Streets, Lanes, And Churches... 10 Dec. Aº Domⁱ. 1666...
John Leake, John Jennings [et. al.] Surveyors." B. M. King's Topographical Collection, xx, no. 17.

CATHEDRAL PROPERTIES
LEASED TO
SEBASTIAN WESTCOTT:

1. Curlowe's House, leased to
   Vicars Choral — 1554/6.
2. "Hospitio and tenement",
   Lovell's Inn.
3. "Four houses".
4. "Eight tenements and a garden".

A SCALE OF YARDS

House.[28] In one way or another none of these proposed building appears to be a convincing site. The petty canons' hall may be ruled out; Westcott was not a minor canon and so would have had no privileges within the college premises; it is also most unlikely that the canons would have tolerated a playhouse in their midst.[29] Not far from the petty canons in the north churchyard was the Almoner's house. Westcott lived there, residing with the choristers and the household staff. He gives the impression in his will that the almonry (in which he died) was merely a residence and a refectory perhaps also a school. As for the parish church of St. Gregory, it had been appropriated to the College of Minor Canons and may well have been the song-school of the almonry boys in earlier times when the Almoner was a member of the college.[30] There is no evidence to show that either Redford or Westcott continued to use the church for their choir practices. Nevertheless "Howes" continuation of Stow's *Annals* (1631) says that the playhouse was the "singing-school."[31] Richard Flecknoe, in *A Short Discourse of the English Stage* (1664), locates the playhouse "behind the Convocation-house," which J. Q. Adams incorrectly places "in or near Paternoster Row."[32] Had the song-school been transferred from the parish church to the Chapter House by Westcott's time?[33] Although it was only a short distance to the east of St. Gregory's in the south churchyard, it seems very doubtful that the great upper

[28]The fullest discussions of the playhouse are by: W. J. Lawrence, *The Elizabethan Playhouse and Other Studies* (1913; reissued, New York, 1963), J. Q. Adams, *Shakespearean Playhouses* (1917; reprinted, Gloucester, Mass., 1960), pp. 111-18; Hillebrand, *op. cit.*, pp. 112-14; and Chambers, II, 10-11, and III, 134-45.

[29]In medieval times the Almoner was a minor canon; the last of such was Thomas Hickman who seemingly relinquished his post as Almoner to become subdean probably between 1528 and 1530. He died in 1534. John Redford, who succeeded Hickman, and Sebastian Westcott, who followed Redford, were both only vicars. By 1574 Westcott was simply the Almoner, for his name was omitted from the list of Vicars Choral. He designates himself as Almoner only in his will.

[30]Chambers (II, 11, n.1.) claims that Stow said that the song-school was housed in St. Gregory's by the twelfth century, but, as Hillebrand points out, such is not Stow's claim.

[31]*Annales, or A General Chronicle of England*, 1631, sig. iiii, I^v, cited by Adams, p. 111, and also by Hillebrand, p. 112.

[32]P. 111, n.3.

[33]W. J. Lawrence, *op. cit.*, p. 25, perhaps in an attempt to reconcile the views of Flecknoe and the *Annales*, describes Paul's playhouse as "in the Choir Singing-School, near the Convocation House."

room where the Dean and Canons met, situated over the open eight-sided undercroft, was used as a singing school. Convocation House seems to be a most unlikely site for a playhouse. The building was octagonal in shape, entirely surrounded by a square, two-storeyed cloister, and completely enclosed from the churchyard by a high wall. The only entrance to it was in the middle of the south transept.[34] Thus, of the possibilities within the churchyard, St. Gregory's Church appears to be the most likely and, furthermore, Hillebrand has shown that in 1598 the church was being used as a schoolhouse, presumably for the education of parish boys.[35] Yet there is reason to be sceptical about this location. Howes alludes to the "singing-school," not to St. Gregory's. Burbage and Heminge refer to Paul's playhouse as "the said house near St. Paul's Church;" they do not mention St. Gregory's,[36] and neither does Stephen Gosson in 1581. If the song-school had been in the church, and if the song-school had been the playhouse, it is odd that a building so venerable, central and well-known as St. Gregory's Church should remain unassociated by name with the playhouse it supposedly housed. Perhaps we should look elsewhere for Westcott's playhouse.

As Almoner, Westcott leased from the Dean and Chapter, at least as early as 1554, three properties immediately outside the walls of the churchyard.[37] Two of these, in Carter Lane and in Sermon Lane, lay scarcely more than fifty yards from the south gate known as Paul's Chain. The four tenements on the corner of Sermon and Carter lanes very possibly housed the ex-choristers who remained with Westcott, since this property was left to the cathedral as a maintenance for senior choristers whose future, after their service in the choir, was not yet settled. The eight tenements and a garden in Carter Lane were situated between Sermon and Dolittle lanes and such a property seems large enough to have housed a small playhouse, especially if we accept Maria Hackett's authority that it was used as a schoolhouse for St. Paul's boys until

---

[34]See the ground plan of Old St. Paul's in *A History of St. Paul's Cathedral*, ed. W. R. Mathews and W. M. Atkins (London, 1964), p. 344.
[35]Pp. 112-13.
[36]In the suit *Keysar and Burbage and Others* (Court of Requests, 1610), privately printed in full by C. W. Wallace (1910), and included in his *Shakespeare and his London Associates*, 1910, p. 95.
[37]See Michael Shaller's Notebook, St. Paul's Cathedral Library, MS. W.D. 32, fol. 67 and *passim*; see also sketch map, p. 29.

the nineteenth century.[38] The third property in Westcott's hands was immediately outside the north churchyard in Lovell's Inn fronting Paternoster Row at the entrance to Paul's Alley which divided the press of buildings in the churchyard and opened to the northwest of the cathedral. Here the Almoner had at his disposal a "hospitio and tenement." Was there a hall here and was this property the site of the playhouse? At any rate the Carter Lane and Paternoster Row locations appear to fit Burbage's and Heminge's descriptions of the playhouse, "the said house near St. Paul's," more aptly than does St. Gregory's Church, and they were both near enough to the almonry to have been conveniently used as a song-school.[39]

Westcott made no direct references to the Paul's playhouse in his will; he did, however, leave small sums of money to "Shep^d [Sheppard?] that kepeth the doore at playes" and to "Pole the keper of the gate." Earlier in the document he had listed bequests to seven or eight ex-choristers and to Peter Phillips, the musician and former chorister, who, it has been suggested above, may have been acting as his assistant music master. Included in this section of the will are bequests to "Thomas Bluet, Thomas Barsey and Robert and John Aunderson nowe remayninge in my house." Were these men associated with Sebastian's theatrical enterprise? The house referred to need not necessarily be taken to be the almonry; it could have been one of the properties outside the churchyard. Certainly the scale of the St. Paul's dramatic activity in the last decade of Westcott's life would suggest that he was unlikely to be operating the company and the playhouse single-handed.

---

[38]Maria Hackett, *Correspondences and Evidences Respecting the Ancient Collegiate School Attached to Saint Paul's Cathedral* (London, 1832), Appendix XII.

[39]Hillebrand (p. 113) draws attention to a statement in J. P. Malcolm's *Londinium Redivivum* (London, 1803), p. 71, which reads: "The house of John Gyles was partly formed by St. Paul's and was 'lately used for a play-house'." Malcolm gives the impression of obtaining the information from MS presentments on visitations at St. Paul's in 1598. Hillebrand's effort to check the accuracy of the claim by a thorough examination of the relevant MS in St. Paul's Library was unsuccessful, and he offers the conjecture that Malcolm may have misread "John" for "Thomas" and thus, perhaps, refers to the incumbent Master of Choristers and Almoner, Thomas Giles. If Hillebrand is correct, Giles would have been administering the same almonry properties as his predecessor, Westcott, and the "house" referred to might well have been one of the properties discussed above.

Of the thirty-two recorded performances of St. Paul's plays under the direction of Westcott the titles of no more than ten are known, and of these only two moralities, *The Marriage of Wit and Science* and *The Contention Between Liberality and Prodigality*, survive in print.[40] At the beginning of his career, Westcott perhaps had in stock for revival the plays written by his friend and predecessor at St. Paul's, John Redford;[41] and since there is evidence of a close association between John Heywood and Westcott up to at least 1559, perhaps Heywood also supplied him with plays. Aside from the performances of the two above-mentioned moral interludes, nothing is known of the plays he presented between 1560 and 1571. Fortunately, we are better informed about the presentations in the last ten years of his career. We may surmise from the description of the plays in the records, inadequate though they often are, that his repertory included moralities (*Liberality and Prodigality* and *The Marriage of Mind and Measure*), tragedies (*Iphigenia* and *Alcmeon*), possibly an adaptation of a Plautine comedy (*Error*), romances from classical pseudo-history and myth (*Titus and Gesippus* and *Cupid and Psyche*) and plays from classical history (*Scipio Africanus* and *Pompey*).

From this it seems clear that the Paul's boys were quick to meet the changing demands of courtly taste in the seventies, replacing moral interludes with the more spectacular plays based upon classical sources which then became a prominent feature of school and chorister performances. Whether or not Westcott was an innovator of this trend, he was its most successful exploiter. No rival company offered so varied a repertory, and this despite the school companies having greater resources of material and personnel. His success may well have been connected with the establishment of his playhouse during these fiercely competitive years. The operation of his own theatre would have allowed him to expand his enterprise and offset the advantages which the schools possessed. There were experienced ex-choristers at hand to supplement the official boys, and, as we have also noticed from the will, a number of men available to aid him. No wonder that Richard Farrant followed suit in 1576.

[40]See Table of Presentations by the Children of Paul's, pp. 34–35.
[41]In addition to *Wit and Science* smaller fragments of two other interludes by Redford are contained in BM MS. Add. 15233, the concluding ten lines of, possibly, a farce and eight lines of another morality.

33

PRESENTATIONS BY THE CHILDREN OF PAUL'S

	Date	Title	Auspice	Presenters	Texts
1.	Winter, 1551-2	Unknown	Princess Elizabeth	Heywood Westcott	—
2.	Easter of May, 1552?	*Nice Wanton?*	King Edward VI	Heywood (Westcott?)	(i) 1560, John King (ii) n.d. [1565?] John Allde
3.	December, 1554 or April, 1557	Unknown	Princess Elizabeth and Queen Mary	Westcott?	—
4.	7 August, 1559	,,	Queen Elizabeth	Heywood, Westcott, Phillips	—
5.	Christmas, 1560	,,	,,	Westcott	—
6.	Christmas, 1561	,,	,,	,,	—
7.	February, 1562	,,	,,	,,	—
8.	Christmas, 1562	,,	,,	,,	—
9.	Christmas, 1564	,,	,,	,,	—
10.	2 February, 1565	,,	,,	,,	—
11. 12. 13. }	Winter, 1565-6	,, ,,	,, Queen Elizabeth and Cecilia of Sweden	,, ,,	— —
14. 15. }	Christmas, 1565	,,	Queen Elizabeth	,,	—
16. 17. }	Christmas – Shrovetide, 1567-8	*Wit and Will* (*The Marriage of Wit and Science*)	,,	,,	n.d. [1569-70], Thomas Marshe

No.	Date	Title			
18.	1 January, 1569	*Prodigality* (*Liberality and Prodigality*)	"	"	1602, Simon Stafford
19.	28 December, 1570	Unknown	"	"	–
20.	25-27 February, 1571	"	"	"	–
21.	28 December, 1571, or 1 January, 1572	*Iphiginia,* "A Tragedie"	"	"	Lost
22.	Christmas—Twelfth Night, 1572-3	Unknown	"	"	–
23.	27 December, 1573	*Alcmeon*	Queen Elizabeth	Westcott	Lost
24.	2 February, 1575	*Liberality and Prodigality* (revival, see no. 17)	"	"	1602, Simon Stafford
25.	6 January, 1576	Unknown	"	"	–
26.	1 January, 1577	*Error*	"	"	Lost
27.	19 February, 1577	*Titus and Gesippus*	"	"	Lost
28.	29 December, 1577	*Cupid and Psyche* (?)	"	"	Lost
29.	1 January, 1579	*The Marriage of Mind and Measure*	"	"	Lost
30.	3 January, 1580	*Scipio Africanus*	"	"	Lost
31.	6 January, 1581	*Pompey*	"	"	Lost
32.	21 December, 1581	Unknown	"	"	–

Other than possibly Redford and Heywood, we do not know who wrote the plays Westcott presented during his long career.[42] There is not a shred of evidence to show that he either composed any music or wrote plays.[43]

Although Westcott's playhouse was older, perhaps by a few years, than Farrant's at the Blackfriars, the records of the City of London should caution us against advancing the claim that it was the first "private" theatre.[44] There are too many proclamations and precepts addressed not only to tavern keepers and innholders, but also to householders, forbidding them to offer performances of plays in their mansions, courts and gardens. Nevertheless, for the moment and so far as we know, it was the first theatre to be settled in a privileged location, to have had a permanent acting and operating company, and to be patronized by a fee-paying public. It is hardly surprising that, in these circumstances, the Children of Paul's was the pre-eminent acting company by the early seventies, and remained so in the lifetime of its director, Sebastian Westcott.[45]

[42]See Arthur Brown, "A Note on Sebastian Westcott and the Plays Presented by the Children of Paul's," *MLQ*, XII (June, 1951), 134-36.

[43]There is, of course, much speculation to the contrary; cf. among others, Hillebrand, *JEGP*, XIV (Oct., 1915); C. W. Roberts, "The Authorship of *Gammer Gurton's Needle*," *PQ*, XIX (April, 1940); J. P. Brawner, "Early Classical Narrative Plays by Sebastian Westcott and Richard Mulcaster," *MLQ*, IV (Dec., 1943), 455-64; Roma Ball, "The Choirboy Actors of St. Paul's Cathedral," *ESRS*, X (June, 1926); and M. C. Bradbrook, " 'Silk? Satin? Kersey? Rags?': The Choristers' Theatre under Elizabeth and James," *SEL*, I (Spring, 1961), 53-64.

[44]See "Dramatic Records of the City of London," Collections, II, Pt. III, *MSR* (1931), pp. 285-320, particularly nos. XX (1558), XXII (1564), XXV (1566), XXIX (1569) and XXXV (1573).

[45]Cf. Irwin Smith, *Shakespeare's Blackfriars Theatre* (New York, 1964), Ch. 6, in which the author fancifully supposes that Farrant's enterprise at the Blackfriars was inspired by James Burbage's intention to build The Theatre (pp. 133-34). If anybody inspired Farrant, it was surely Westcott, a fellow Master of the Choristers and his foremost rival as play presenter at Court. When he died his overseer and "deere freende m^r Henrye Evans" took in hand the task of promoting the company Westcott had directed in the theatre Farrant had built.

Tragedy at the Children's Theatres after 1600: A Challenge to the Adult Stage

R. A. FOAKES

It is now a commonplace of theatre history that something like a revolution occurred on the London stage in the late 1950s, when, it seemed, the well-made play portraying genteel, public-school, upper middle-class characters and manners, like *The Deep Blue Sea* (1952), and the modish verse plays of Christopher Fry (*The Dark Is Light Enough*, 1954), and T. S. Eliot (*The Confidential Clerk*, 1954), simultaneously fell out of fashion. What happened has been summed up by John Russell Taylor in this way:

> ... in May 1956 came *Look Back in Anger*. No need to rehearse again the brilliant history of British drama in the next decade. John Osborne's impassioned monologue plays; the intense, finely chiselled works of Harold Pinter; the rough, well-meaning social dramas of Arnold Wesker; the obsessive, loose-jointed farces of Henry Livings; the intellectual teasings of N. F. Simpson; the voluble, extravagant tragi-comedies of John Arden; the patterns of sounds and actions elaborated by Ann Jellicoe; the director's field-days Joan Littlewood had with Brendan Behan and Shelagh Delaney. It has been rich, strange, infinitely various.[1]

No simple explanation for this abrupt change towards a new realism, a drama of the absurd, and a drama of political engagement

[1]*The Rise and Fall of the Well-made Play* (1967), pp. 161-62.

can be given. Political circumstances, changing social conditions, new opportunities in the theatre, the productions of Ionesco's *The Lesson* and Beckett's *Waiting for Godot* in London in 1955, the visit there of the Berliner Ensemble in 1956, may all be significant; but finally there is no way of accounting for the explosion of new and very talented dramatists after 1956. Two features of this change, or series of changes, in the mood of the London theatres are, however, worth noting. One is indicated by the author of the passage quoted, who goes on to observe that many plays which appear revolutionary may be seen less as a repudiation of the well-made play than as a transformation of it, so that what is most new in recent drama has nevertheless roots in old fashions and traditions. The other feature is the persistence throughout the 1950s and 1960s of older modes of drama, as instanced in the enormously long run of the old-fashioned whodunnit, *The Mousetrap*. The "revolution" that brought Pinter and Arden to the fore may have been the most exciting and the dominant movement in the period, but it did not by any means do away with even the kinds of play it seemed to be displacing.

I instance this period of sudden change in the contemporary theatre not to press a close analogy, but indirectly to support a hypothesis about an earlier period on the London stage, roughly the decade 1600-1610. The further back we travel mentally in time, the greater the effort of imagination required to realize that a span of ten years is a long time to those living through it, and may seem to them full of novelty and change. Distinctions tend to dissolve, and changes to go unnoticed, in the broad perspective of the history of the Elizabethan and Jacobean stage. In this perspective the revival of the children's companies at St. Paul's and Blackfriars in 1599 or 1600, and their success for a brief period, challenging the adult companies, may slip readily into an image of two rival traditions, each throwing up a homogeneous body of drama, and each opposed to the other. This is the picture drawn in Alfred Harbage's influential account of the matter:

> Fifty-five extant plays can be assigned with confidence to the côterie theatres between 1599 and 1613. . . . The most striking thing about the list is the overwhelming preponderance of satirical comedies, all but about a dozen of the total being classifiable as such. Most of the rest are tragedies or tragicomedies. Chronicle plays and romances are at a complete discount. Classical stories and settings have, in

the main, been abandoned, but the classical allegiances of the authors are in evidence. . . . In all but a few of the plays the theme is sexual transgression, coupled in tragedy with treachery and murder, and in comedy with cupidity and fraud. It is a body of drama preoccupied with lust and murder or lust and money, and with the exhibition of the foolish and the foul.[2]

No doubt the "body of drama" described by John Russell Taylor, and which seemed to him "rich, strange, infinitely various," will, in the long perspective of historians writing three hundred years hence, be reduced to a similar homogeneity, and classified in general terms; for the time being, however, as we see it, so to speak in close-up, it appears "infinitely various." It is, I think, vitally important to recover this close view as far as possible if we are to understand what was happening in earlier periods.

A closer view of what Harbage calls the "côterie theatres" suggests a very different and much more complicated picture than the one he drew. The hypothesis I wish to propose arises especially from a study of the handful of tragedies performed by the boys, but the shifts and changes shown in the development of tragedy at the children's theatres could equally be illustrated from an analysis of the satirical comedies they played. In simple outline the hypothesis is this: that the revival of the children's theatres in 1599/1600 soon made a great impact on the London theatre as a whole, and challenged the adult stages strongly enough to force them to take over and use in their own way styles and techniques of drama first exploited in the plays put on by the boys; that in order to maintain their challenge to the older and more solidly established adult theatres, the children and their dramatists were driven, especially at first, to bold experiment; and that, during the decade following their revival, the children's theatres and the dramatists who wrote for them formed a major influence in determining the course English drama was to take.[3] These years saw, I think, many new changes and developments, and must have seemed to offer great

---

[2]*Shakespeare and the Rival Traditions* (1952, reprinted 1968), p. 71.
[3]This is in direct opposition to the view of David Frost in *The School of Shakespeare* (1968), who argues that the influence of Shakespeare was pervasive, that Shakespeare "resurrected" the Romance and the Revenge play, and that "Marston, Fletcher and Middleton in the early part of their careers all produced imitations or continuations of Shakespeare" (p. 246). Mr. Frost is not concerned with the differences between the theatres, or between companies of actors, and too often his evidence is very thin, and his chronology dubious.

variety to a constant theatregoer; the children and their writers were the initiators usually, as in demonstrating the possibilities for combining satire and tragedy, or for exploiting consciously an awareness of the actor as actor, so perhaps creating a theatrical basis for the success of formal tragicomedy and the heroic play. It seems to have happened that experiments in the boy's theatres tended to lead, if anywhere, to masterpieces in the adult theatre; and the failure of the children's theatres to produce any plays of first distinction has led to their brief flourishing being seen as a kind of footnote to the continuing stream of major drama, so that their importance needs to be emphasized the more strongly.

In order to argue in this way, it is not necessary to dismiss Harbage's general statement as simply false. Indeed, he was merely rephrasing H. N. Hillebrand's comment on the children's companies, that they pursued "an unrelenting and unparalleled course of satire."[4] This in turn might claim authority from Thomas Heywood's remarks in his *Apology for Actors* (1612), where he attacks the abuse "lately crept" into the profession of acting, in satirizing "the state, the court, the law," and expresses disapproval, especially in relation to the boy-actors:

> The liberty which some arrogate to themselves, committing their bitterness, and liberal invectives against all estates, to the mouths of children, supposing their juniority to be a privilege for any railing, be it never so violent, I could advise all such, to curb and limit this presumed liberty within the bands of discretion and government.[5]

The boys clearly had a gift for acting satire. This seems to have had to do with their difference from the adult players, and the sense in which these "little eyases" and "rascally tits"[6] were mimicking rather than simply representing men on the stage. They were known as "children," a name which emphasizes their "juniority" and their difference, and their repertory was clearly geared to what they could do well. This is only to say that their range was more limited than that of the adult players, but it was still wide enough to have great variety, even within the spectrum of possibilities offered by satire and plays giving them opportunities for "railing."

[4]H. N. Hillebrand, *The Child Actors* (1926, reprinted 1964), p. 270.
[5]Cited in E. K. Chambers, *The Elizabethan Stage* (1923), IV, 253, and in G. E. Bentley, *The Seventeenth-Century Stage* (1968), p. 21.
[6]The phrases are from Hamlet, II.ii.342, and from the Induction to Ben Jonson's *Cynthia's Revels*, 121.

Recently students of what has become known, in Harbage's terms, as "côterie drama," have emphasized its "deliberate self-consciousness,"[7] and the exploitation in the plays performed by the boys of a "dual consciousness of the actors as actors and characters."[8] To draw out and establish this important feature of many plays put on at Paul's and Blackfriars also tends to strengthen a single overall image of their repertory, their technique, and the idea that "the private playhouses had developed a distinctive idea of theatre by the time Shakespeare became associated with Blackfriars, with a dramaturgy which was recognizably different from that at the Globe."[9] However true this claim may be, it is a general one, and tells us nothing about the struggles and experiments of the children's theatres from year to year. The history of these remains, of course, obscure, but some facts can be established to suggest, at the very least, a good deal of change at the management level. The history of the Paul's boys, who seem to have ceased playing by the end of 1606, offers little to go on, except for the withdrawal of John Marston about 1603-4, who thenceforth became poet to the company at Blackfriars. The history of the Blackfriars company is better documented, and is marked by lawsuits, new agreements, and changes of managership. The promoters of the company that began playing in September 1600, Henry Evans and Nathaniel Giles, brought in new partners in 1602, and again in 1604. One of these, Edward Kirkham, moved over to Paul's by 1605, after Marston's transfer the other way. In 1604 the poet Samuel Daniel became licenser of plays to the company when they were authorized to call themselves the Children of the Queen's Revels. In the next few years a series of difficulties beset the company, and several of their plays gave offence; Chapman's *Tragedy of Byron* provoked the wrath of King James in 1608, and another lost play attacked the King personally; there followed a restraint on playing, and the dissolution of the company. Reconstituted under new management, and regaining the royal patronage, lost apparently as a result of the

---

[7]Arthur Kirsch, "*Cymbeline* and Coterie Dramaturgy," *ELH*, XXXIV (1967), 286.
[8]Michael Shapiro, "Children's Troupes: Dramatic Illusion and Acting Style," *Comparative Drama*, III (1967), 48.
[9]Kirsch, *loc. cit.*, pp. 285-86. It is fair to add that this essay offers an important argument about the influence of the private theatres on Shakespeare, and Michael Shapiro attempts to show that the companies of child-actors used several styles of acting. Both essays seek to draw general conclusions, but both in their different ways also reinforce my argument.

offence given by *Eastward Ho!* in 1605, they became known as the Children of the Queen's Revels at Whitefriars, succeeding another shadowy company of boys known as the Children of the King's Revels, which played there from about 1607 to 1609.[10] By this time, however, the boys were themselves becoming men, and I am concerned only with the companies at Paul's and Blackfriars.

The sense of frequent change in management, and of a succession of crises in their affairs, which the known history of the Blackfriars company suggests, does not in itself point to corresponding changes in repertory or in technique. The known facts about this company and the Paul's boys do, however, chime in with other evidence to indicate a series of changes here as well. At first there seems to have been a period of adjustment when the boys began playing under new professional management in 1599 and 1600. They revived old plays like Lyly's *Love's Metamorphosis* and *The Wisdom of Doctor Dodypoll*, plays referred to satirically in *Jack Drum's Entertainment* as "musty fopperies of antiquity."[11] This short phase seems to have been followed at Paul's by burlesques of adult styles and adult players, notably in *Jack Drum's Entertainment, Histriomastix* and *Antonio and Mellida*, and John Marston may rapidly have become the presiding genius, the first new successful dramatist, for the Paul's boys. Blackfriars seems to have preferred humour plays like Chapman's *Sir Giles Goosecap* and court comedies like *Cynthia's Revels*. The onset of plague and the restraint on playing in March 1603 seem to have brought important changes. At this time Marston became a partner in the Blackfriars company, and a writer for them. After the resumption of playing in April 1604, a more realistic vein of city comedy began to dominate at both theatres, but even within these generally satirical plays a great variety can be seen, in style, theme, and in moral tone. T. M. Parrott may have been too categorical in associating their arrival on the stage with the success of *Westward Ho!* played at Paul's in 1604, especially in view of the difficulty of dating accurately some of Middleton's comedies; nevertheless his account is substantially true. Noting that the Blackfriars company immediately met the

[10]H. N. Hillebrand's *The Child Actors* remains the best and fullest account of these companies, supplementing the work of Chambers in *The Elizabethan Stage*, II, 8-61. I am only concerned with those matters that bear on my general argument.
[11]Cited from *The Plays of John Marston*, edited H. Harvey Wood (1939), III, 234.

challenge of *Westward Ho!* with *Eastward Ho!* early in 1605, he says, "There is not a trace before *Eastward Ho!* of the realistic comedy of manners of London life" on the stage at Blackfriars. Before this he could find only "comedy of courtly life, enlivened by 'humours' and personal satire, adaptations of Latin and Italian comedies, romantic comedy and tragi-comedy, and a single specimen of classical tragedy."[12] These two plays certainly opened up new possibilities for the children's companies, who found in these city comedies a kind of play well suited to their talents.[13]

These variations and developments in the comedies played by the children are matched by changes in their mode of tragedy, changes which are all the more striking in that so few tragedies known to have been played by them survive. The only one that can with certainty be assigned to the period before 1603 is *Antonio's Revenge*, written by John Marston for Paul's, but the children at Blackfriars played *The Spanish Tragedy* or some version of an Hieronimo play, since the King's Men stole *The Malcontent* in retaliation. After the long interruption in playing between March 1603 and April 1604, Samuel Daniel was appointed licenser of plays for the Blackfriars company, and it may be that his play *Philotas* was performed by them as a result of this. In his apology prefixed to the published text, Daniel says that it was largely written in 1600; politically it caused a stir, as it appeared to allude to the conspiracy of the Earl of Essex, but dramatically it is an oddity, as a deliberately classical tragedy with formal choruses. The tragedies written for the children after 1603-4 differ from Marston's early plays in having much more clearly a serious intention. First came Marston's *Sophonisba* and Chapman's *Bussy D'Ambois*, between 1604 and 1606, then Chapman's *Conspiracy and Tragedy of Byron*, of about 1608. Three later plays written for the private theatre, Chapman's *Revenge of Bussy D'Ambois*, Marston's *Insatiate Countess*, and *Cupid's Revenge* by Beaumont and Fletcher, all dating from about 1610-12, are perhaps not strictly to be thought of as children's plays and I shall not deal with these. In

[12]T. M. Parrott, *The Plays and Poems of George Chapman: The Comedies* (1910), p. 840.

[13]This is a narrower conception of city comedy than that employed by Brian Gibbons in his recent book *Jacobean City Comedy* (1968). This book is in fact concerned with satirical comedy generally in the period from 1597 onwards, including comedy of humours, and its main effort is to indicate the social and economic background, and to describe the plays from a literary point of view.

addition, a little aside from the mainstream, John Mason wrote *The Turk*, a young man's energetic and derivative play, for the King's Revels at Whitefriars about 1607-9.

An acute apologist for Marston as a dramatist with a serious ethical intention in *Antonio's Revenge* has noticed two features of the play; first, the detached, satiric portraiture and the "philosophic stances which comment on one another, but never really engage or necessarily issue into action," and second, that "It is one of the principal difficulties of *Antonio's Revenge* that the surface language of conventional moral concern is not merely detached from but largely contradictory of the underlying pattern of amoral ritual."[14] This is well said, but both features could be interpreted differently, as positive aspects of a satiric and mocking design, exposing to a detached and comically horrible scrutiny conventional moral concerns. I believe this to be the correct interpretation, and as the question has been debated elsewhere in print, I shall merely draw attention to some other aspects of the play which have not been much noticed.[15] The play exaggerates to the point of absurdity features of earlier revenge plays, offering the child-actors much pompous rant and "braggart passion" to declaim. In particular, it magnifies all the more lurid effects of *The Spanish Tragedy*, from the opening scene, when Piero the villain enters "smear'd in blood, a poniard in one hand bloody, and a torch in the other, Strotzo following him with a cord," to the final scene, in which the conspirators "pluck out" Piero's tongue, and "triumph over him." It also uses, and overdoes to the point of parody, the rhetorical devices of Senecan tragedy. The stage directions, which are presumably Marston's own, require a series of sensational effects designed to shock, like the discovery of Feliche's body, hung up and "stabb'd thick with wounds" (I.ii.193), or the revelation of the ghost of Andrugio sitting on the bed of Maria (III.ii.61). The shock of sensational or gruesome effect can also turn into a moral shock, as in the centrepiece of the play, the extraordinary scene in "Saint

[14]Citing respectively G. K. Hunter, "English Folly and Italian Vice: The Moral Landscape of John Marston," in *Jacobean Theatre* (Stratford-upon-Avon Studies, I, edited J. R. Brown and Bernard Harris, 1960), p. 91; and *Antonio's Revenge*, edited G. K. Hunter (1965), p. xviii.

[15]See the essays by G. K. Hunter mentioned in the previous note; also Anthony Caputi, *John Marston, Satirist* (1961) and R. A. Foakes, "John Marston's Fantastical Plays: *Antonio and Mellida* and *Antonio's Revenge*," *Philological Quarterly*, XLI (1962), 229-39. Alvin Kernan, *The Cankered Muse* (1959), pp. 206-18, is also relevant.

Mark's Church" at dead of night (III.i), in which Antonio watches at the tomb of his father, sees his father's ghost rise up crying revenge and murder, and ends by stabbing the boy Julio, Piero's son, and sprinkling blood over the tomb. He goes off crying,

> Lo, thus I heave my blood-dyed hands to Heaven;
> Even like insatiate hell, still crying, "More!
> My heart hath thirsting dropsies after gore."
> Sound peace and rest to church, night-ghosts and graves;
> Blood cries for blood; and murder murder craves. (III.i.211)

The peculiar frisson this may have given the original audience is hard to recover. The actor playing Antonio was himself a choirboy attached to the cathedral of Saint Paul's, and the play was performed in the precincts, possibly in a building forming part of the cathedral complex,[16] so that "Saint Paul's" echoed underneath "Saint Mark's." The most horrifying vengeance Laertes could imagine to take upon the murderer of his father would be "To cut his throat i' th' church" (*Hamlet,* IV.vii.126); the actor-choirboy Antonio goes beyond this, for he stabs an innocent boy in church, and there heaves his "blood-dyed hands to heaven."

At the same time we are not allowed to take this very seriously because the play is designed as a vehicle for child-actors consciously ranting in oversize parts. Their grand speeches do not spring from a developed emotional situation, and are undermined by discontinuities, incongruous juxtapositions, effects of bathos, and parody, so that we are not moved, but rather encouraged to maintain a detachment from them. It is a constant aspect of Marston's technique in this play that it simultaneously inflates, in tragic hyperbole, and diminishes, in the figures of child-actors strutting, the stock idea of hero and villain. The self-consciousness of the actors about their roles, as when Alberto and Pandulfo sit down to "talk as chorus to this tragedy" (I.ii.299), contributes to this effect, and the frequent presence of the fool Balurdo undermines some of the more "solemn" moments, as when Antonio's dream, horribly stuffed with omens of dread, is absurdly echoed in Balurdo's dream of "the abominable ghost of a misshapen simile" (I.ii.103-34). The many echoes, quotations, and repetitions of stage effects from Kyd and Seneca are changed or exaggerated to suggest a mockery of

---

[16]The exact location where the Paul's boys played is not known, but it was "near St. Paule's church" (see E. K. Chambers, *The Elizabethan Stage,* II, 22), and may have been in St. Gregory's Church, which abutted onto the nave.

conventional tragic attitudes; perhaps the children and their audiences took pleasure in the way Marston plays with familiar rhetorical patterns and familiar authors. So Antonio enters in II.ii with a book of Seneca's philosophical writing in imitation of Hieronimo's entry carrying a volume of Seneca's plays (*The Spanish Tragedy*, III.xiii). Antonio rejects Seneca's preaching of patience in *De Providentia*, preferring to be "fir'd with impatience," while Hieronimo, rejecting the exhortations of Agamemnon to "strike home," seeks to subject his "heart to patience." Each then, however, reverses his position; Antonio ends the scene a "prostrate wretch" lying full of woe as if "on his tomb," while Hieronimo goes off in a passion for revenge.

Here Antonio merely reverses and exaggerates the change of mood, but such reversals and exaggerations can be used to a more potent effect. Perhaps the best example is another echo of *The Spanish Tragedy* in the initial entry of Piero with bloody arms, and carrying a poniard and a torch, followed by Strotzo with a cord. This recalls, but with the addition of the blood and the torch, the entry of Hieronimo "with a poniard in one hand and a rope in the other" (III.xii). Hieronimo is contemplating suicide, Piero congratulating himself on the murder of Feliche, and Marston has made the effect even more sensational. But not content with one use of it, he goes on to employ it again in III.ii, where this time Antonio comes on stage "his arms bloody, a torch and a poniard." This can only be intended as a deliberate shock; Piero, the villain, came on rejoicing in the death of Feliche, and now Antonio triumphs in the slaying of the boy Julio. Their deeds are made visually identical, and Marston equates his villain and his hero. At the end of the play Piero is cruelly killed after his tongue has been plucked out, and after Antonio has offered him a Thyestean feast of the limbs of his dead son. As the killers now boast and wrangle about which of them actually murdered Piero, they are greeted, to their amazement, by some senators as saviours, "Religiously held sacred," and they go off finally to live

> enclos'd
> In holy verge of some religious order,
> Most constant votaries. (V.iii.151)

The flouting of moral consistency goes together with another reminder that the actors are choirboys playing in the "holy verge" of

Saint Paul's. This last scene is consciously outrageous, mocking with calculated enormity a conventional ending which would have punished Antonio.

If a serious purpose is to be found here, it is best defined in terms of an interest in "the cold realities of power,"[17] the rejection or distortion of accepted values, so that the heroic certainties, the clear oppositions of plays like *The Spanish Tragedy* or *Hamlet*, are made to look old-fashioned. However, the main impact of the play is melodramatic and satirical, and the satire is directed less against folly and vice than against conventional literary and theatrical styles, attitudes and moral patterns. Because of this it was an achievement of a sort that could not be repeated, though its innovations of technique and attitude made a significant impact on later plays. At some time between 1600 and 1604, when *The Malcontent* was published, the new style of Marston was heard on the stage of the Globe theatre. For their performance of this play, Shakespeare's company provided additions to take the place of the interludes of music customary in the children's theatres. The additions, written by John Webster, include an Induction in which one actor, Sinklo, bets that "the play is not so well acted as it hath been," and a number of passages which expand the comic dialogue in the play by adding a fool, Passarello, and elaborating the part of the old corrupt courtier Bilioso. The additions also provide more for Burbage, who played Malevole, to speak, chiefly in exchanges with Passarello and Bilioso, but also by enlarging one or two of his big speeches in the opening and closing scenes. Both the Induction, which calls attention to the artifice of the play, and the other additions expanding the foolery in the action seemed designed to reinforce the comic, even absurd mood which the children could establish naturally by aping adult actors.

If these elements, like Marston's address to the reader and the prologue, all emphasize that the play is a comedy, and the author's pen "still must write of fools, whiles't writes of men," nevertheless it seems, like *Antonio's Revenge*, to point the way to a satirical mode of tragedy, rather than to developments in comedy. The idea of the Duke in disguise watching over the corruptions in his state links the play with *Measure for Measure*, but this is not an important connection. It may be more properly seen as looking forward

[17]G. K. Hunter, "English Folly and Italian Vice," p. 91.

47

to *The Revenger's Tragedy,* but it is important to notice its limitations in this respect. After the brilliant outrageousness of the *Antonio* plays Marston seems steadily to have drawn in his horns. *The Malcontent* is in some ways an advance. Malevole nicely draws into one role Antonio and Balurdo, combining something of the grandiose heroic stance of the one with the grotesque foolery of the other; it may be that Burbage made something of this character, passionate, melancholy, stoic and absurd by turns, but the play is clearly designed to prevent us from taking him or it too seriously. The main interest is in intrigue; the insistence on the externality of the action, the intricate arrangements of effects, as in the use of multiple disguises, the conscious staging, and the exaggerations of the language all establish a tonality that undermines Malevole's attacks on court-corruption and his enthusiasm for "fearless virtue" (I.iv.13).

It seems to me doubtful whether this play really evokes a "sense of moral distress," or provides a "successful fusion of the solemn and grotesque,"[18] as has been claimed for it. The ingenuity of the action always seems more interesting than its moral nature. Malevole, the disguised Duke of Genoa, claims to be an Asper playing the role of Macilente:

> Hope, hope, that never forsak'st the wretched'st man,
> Yet bidd'st me live and lurk in this disguise:
> What, play I well the free-breath'd discontent?
> Why, man, we are all philosophical monarchs
> Or natural fools. Celso, the court's afire;
> The duchess' sheets will smoke for't ere it be long.
> Impure Mendoza, that sharp-nos'd lord, that made
> The cursed match link'd Genoa with Florence,
> Now broad-horns the duke, which he now knows.
> Discord to malcontents is very manna;
> When the ranks are burst, then scuffle, Altofront. (I.iv.29)

Something serious could have been made of the clash between his claim to be a "philosophical monarch" superior to the folly of others, and his enjoyment of lust in others, his delight in discord. In fact the two stances remain separate, and the second one provides the prevailing note of the play. In this Malevole is seconded by Mendoza, who is also contriving discord in the court usurped

18The phrases are from Anthony Caputi, *John Marston, Satirist,* pp. 196 and 198.

by Pietro. So now when Malevole informs Pietro that he is being cuckolded by Mendoza, he does not know that Ferneze has replaced Mendoza in the affections of Aurelia. Marston is thus able to create two fine melodramatic scenes, one in which Mendoza is confronted by Pietro with drawn sword, and jests his way out of death to persuade Pietro that Ferneze is the man:

> *Enter* Pietro, *his sword drawn*
> Pietro: A mischief fill thy throat, thou foul-jaw'd slave!
>   Say thy prayers.
> Mendoza: I ha' forgot 'em.
> Pietro: Thou shalt die!
> Mendoza: So shalt thou. I am heart-mad.
> Pietro: I am horn-mad.
> Mendoza: Extreme mad.
> Pietro: Monstrously mad.
> Mendoza: Why?
> Pietro: Why? Thou, thou hast dishonoured my bed. (I.vii.1)

Whether Mendoza's replies here be taken as impudent, or mocking, or careless, they effectively empty the situation of danger and expose Pietro's stance as ineffective; if Mendoza were in immediate danger of death, he would not reply so wittily to "Thou shalt die" with a reminder that all men must eventually, "So shalt thou."

The other scene is that in which Ferneze comes out of Aurelia's bedroom to be "received" on the sword of Mendoza (II.v), and drops "dead" before Aurelia on the stage. Mendoza stays to convince Aurelia that Pietro is to blame for this, and they conspire together to murder Pietro "Instantly" (1.74). Mendoza then employs Malevole to bury the body of Ferneze, but as soon as Malevole is left alone on stage, Ferneze, who has been lying there "dead" for 140 lines, comes to life, and turns out to be merely wounded after all. This provides an occasion for Malevole to preach against lust:

> But fame ne'er heals, still rankles worse and worse;
> Such is of uncontrolled lust the curse.
> Think what it is in lawless sheets to lie;
> But, O, Ferneze, what in lust to die! (II.v.146)

The sermon bears little relation to the action. Ferneze's offence is to have slept with Aurelia, who already commits adultery with Mendoza, and whose virtue is as easy as that of Maquerelle and her ladies of the court; "fame" in this court appears to lie in the number of conquests a man or woman can make rather than in a chaste life. This is no rape, and cannot be taken seriously as adultery; and Ferneze shows no concern for his fame, while, for all their talk of murder, neither Mendoza or Pietro can ever manage to carry one out. The moral implications of each situation tend to evaporate, and we are left with fine theatrical moments and entertaining, sometimes absurd, intrigues.

These reach a climax when, in IV.iv, Malevole and Pietro, now disguised as a hermit, confront one another, and discover that they have each been hired by Pietro to kill the other by the same means and at the same time:

> *Malevole*: How do you? How dost, duke?
> *Pietro*: O, let the last day fall! Drop, drop on our cursed heads! Let heaven unclasp itself, vomit forth flames.
> *Malevole*: O, do not rand, do not turn player. There's more of them than can well live one by another already. What, art an infidel still?
> *Pietro*: I am amaz'd, struck in a swoon with wonder. I am commanded to poison thee.
> *Malevole*: I am commanded to poison thee at supper.
> *Pietro*: At supper?
> *Malevole*: In the citadel.
> *Pietro*: In the citadel?
> *Malevole*: Cross-capers! Tricks!

The effect of this is surely intended to be comic, to draw attention to the "cross-capers," as Malevole stops Pietro from ranting with a gratuitous joke about actors in London; at the same time, by exposing Pietro's outcry as bombast, Malevole is also discouraging the audience from taking him seriously when he "turns player" a little later in the scene to declaim,

> World! 'Tis the only region of death, the greatest shop of the devil, the cruel'st prison of men, out of the which none pass without paying their dearest breath for a fee. . . . (IV.iv.27)

Indeed, such pronouncements, expressions of Malevole's melancholy and moral indignation, are to a large extent subverted by the nature of the play, its comic tone, its tendency to relax and play with situations, to exploit intrigue and melodrama for their own sakes, to be too conscious of itself; no one suffers much because in the context no one sins much in a world where no one thinks twice about lust or murder, and though much is intended, little in fact happens. Malevole's perfunctory moral comment at the end (expanded by Webster), and his quick dispensation of rewards and punishments, count for little except as a winding up of the action. One wonders what he will now do for entertainment in Genoa, and his wife Maria, at last released after a long, chaste, and dull imprisonment, seems merely to have missed all the fun.

If *The Malcontent* looks back to Kyd and Seneca, it also points forward to satirical tragedies played by the adult companies. It cannot be dated precisely, but was certainly acted by the children at Blackfriars before the King's Men stole it, and Marston may have taken it with him when he transferred from Paul's to Blackfriars. It is not possible to say whether it was written before or after Jonson's *Sejanus*, but certainly these two plays, like *The Revenger's Tragedy*, were all performed at the Globe between 1603 and 1606. In a sense these all stem from Marston's influence, and they brought home on the stage of the leading adult company the potentialities for a new kind of tragedy. Each of them exploits a satirical distancing of its action in a different way; *The Malcontent* seems in the end to be self-consciously playing with theatrical effects; *Sejanus* offers a bleak vision of a world wholly given over to intrigue and murder for political ends, but distanced and so made endurable through the satirical perspective provided by a group of commentators; *The Revenger's Tragedy* integrates the witty detachment that becomes an end in itself in Marston's plays into a new mode of satirical tragedy, in which the protagonist's sardonic stance is made to take effect fully as a part of the play's serious action. During these same years Shakespeare seems to have been influenced by the new satire of the children's stages in writing the "dark" comedies, and in the final version of *Hamlet*, published in 1604-5.[19] Perhaps he absorbed more cautiously the new spirit, which finds expression less in the four central heroic tragedies than in *Timon of Athens* and *Coriolanus*.

One other play that should be mentioned here is Chettle's *Hoff-*

[19]The relation of *Antonio's Revenge* and *The Malcontent* to *Hamlet* is a difficult and much debated question. I assume here that the text of the good Quarto of Hamlet, published in late 1604 or early 1605, represents a late stage in the evolution of the play; and even if the first version of *Hamlet* preceded the other two plays, nevertheless the text we have is a late one, and may well have been influenced by them.

man, probably belonging to 1602, though not published until 1631. This is usually assigned to an adult company because Chettle usually wrote for the Admiral's Men, but the play is similar in many ways to *Antonio's Revenge*, with a good deal of self-conscious rant and hyperbole, which suggests a play for the children, as does the way it jests with its own mode, especially in the figures of the foolish Jerome and Stilt. What the Blackfriars boys did with *Hieronimo* or *The Spanish Tragedy* we cannot know, but the signs are that in discovering how to mock the heroic and the revenge traditions of tragedy, and use these for satirical, grotesque, or even comic purposes, they gave a lead which the adult companies followed; and in doing this *Antonio's Revenge* appears to be a seminal play. If possibly in *Hoffman*, but certainly by 1604-6 with *Sejanus* and *The Revenger's Tragedy*, the adult players were taking over and making their own what the boys had initiated and, what is more, achieving near-masterpieces, this may account in large measure for the change in the style of tragedy offered by the children's theatres after the plague year. Daniel's *Philotas* could be a sport, though it might also be an attempt at something different; but there is no doubt that Marston's *Sophonisba* and Chapman's *Bussy D'Ambois* represent something new.

Marston's play refers to *Sejanus* (printed in 1605) in its note to the reader claiming that the author has not laboured "to tie myself to anything as an historian but to enlarge everything as a Poet." It had been promised in the address to the reader prefixed to *The Fawn*, printed in the same year as *Sophonisba* (1606), where Marston apologizes for the slightness of that comedy, and promises to "present a tragedy to you which shall boldly abide the most curious perusal." Like *The Dutch Courtesan*, printed in 1605, *The Fawn* states on the title page that it was played by the children of the Queen's Revels, whereas the title page of *Sophonisba* merely refers to Blackfriars. Because of this, *Sophonisba* is often dated in 1606, on the grounds that the Queen's patronage was withdrawn from the company at the end of 1605; but as it was printed after the others, the title page may merely show that the author or publisher was being a little more careful. All it proves is that the play was published after the Queen dissociated herself from the company. Chapman's *Bussy D'Ambois*, printed in 1607 and played by the Paul's boys, is equally hard to date accurately, and is commonly assigned to 1604 because of the phrase "Tis leap year"

(I.ii.81), which need not be taken as referring to the year of composition at all. Both plays, it is generally agreed, belong to the period after the resumption of playing in 1604, can be roughly dated 1604-05, and can be regarded as contemporary with one another. Both indeed may have originated with the Queen's Revels in 1604, although *Bussy* was later acted at Paul's.

In an epistle to the reader, Marston apologizes for the "fashion of the Entrances and Music" of his play, for "it is printed only as it was presented by youths, & after the fashion of the private stage." In fact, the entrances and other directions, which appear to be the author's, are invaluable not only as evidence of possible theatrical practice on the "private stage," but also, and more importantly, because they tell us much about the essential nature of *Sophonisba*. The play is notable for the full directions indicating a clever use of dumbshows, processions, marches, masques, and other stage movements of a stylized kind, and these evidently contribute much to the play. What they contribute is suggested by the stage direction in III.i, "Cornets and Organs playing full music. Enters the solemnity of a sacrifice. . . ." This "solemnity," or observance of ceremony and ritual, is a feature of the action, from the opening of Masinissa and Sophonisba on one side of the stage, opposed to Syphax on the other, with the Prologue speaking from between them. Other directions confirm the sense of things happening "in full state," to cite Scipio's entry in Act V, where incidentally another "solemnity" comes on stage as Masinissa brings forward the body of the dead Sophonisba. The pattern of "solemnity" controls the stage action visually, within a framework of ceremonial and ritual, so stylizing it. This is an important form of aesthetic control imposed on the play.

I think that if one simply read the text, paying little attention to the staging, one might be inclined to share Hillebrand's view that here, as in Chapman's tragedy, the children are "playing with fire and thunder, in which fine passages and noble lines cannot successfully combat the general unreality."[20] But Hillebrand did not observe the ceremonial formality shaping the play's action. He also ignored another characteristic, namely its epic quality. For, like Chapman in *Bussy D'Ambois*, Marston is in this play closer to Marlowe than to Kyd or Seneca, at any rate in the overall design

[20]H. N. Hillebrand, *The Child Actors*, p. 272.

of the play. I do not wish to suggest a close link here; indeed a careful distinction needs to be made between the fluidity of Marlowe's lines in *Tamburlaine*, with their frequent return to a three-stressed line, and the deliberately heavy and slow rhythm of Marston's verse, which has a far more static quality. Marston uses epic simile, a range of rhetorical devices, and a fair amount of rhyme, to elevate the tone and magnify his characters into statuesque figures speaking high astounding terms. At the same time, the undercurrent of mockery found in *Antonio's Revenge* or even in *The Malcontent*, and the self-conscious, joking exposure of rant in these plays for what it is, are not to be found in *Sophonisba*. The ceremony of the action is matched by the ceremony of the verse, which can accommodate comfortably such a catalogue of personifications as this from the description of Scipio in I.ii:

> Before whose brows flight and disorder hurry,
> With whom march burnings, murder, wrong, waste, rapes,
> Behind whom a sad train is seen, woe, fears,
> Tortures, Lean Need, Famine and helpless tears.

The verse here, as often, slips into the clinch of a couplet, as if to emphasize its special kind of artificiality. Of course it is "unreal" in Hillebrand's terms; it had to be for boys to attempt to present epic heroes.

Precisely this "unreality" enables Marston to employ his strangest effects. I mean such incidents as Syphax haling in Sophonisba by the hair in III.i; "his dagger twone about her hair," he drags her on stage, and threatens violent rape. Later, thwarted by her determined chastity, he invokes the hellish witch Erichtho, who promises to make her love him, and in fact deceives him by passing herself off as Sophonisba. The sexual violence of these scenes is new and remarkable, making such attempts on chastity in contemporary plays as those by Volpone on Celia, or by the disguised Vindice and Lussurioso on Castiza in *The Revenger's Tragedy*, seem tame by comparison. Twice Syphax makes an attempt on Sophonisba, and she eludes him, the first time by escaping through a vault. Twice he leaps lustifully into bed, once to find his drunken servant Vanque substituted for Sophonisba, the second time to make love to Erichtho disguised as Sophonisba. These incidents, however, which in themselves might seem merely sensational, are held within the ritualistic structure of the play. Before Syphax makes his first attempt on Sophonisba, she asks for time to make a sacrifice, and in a solemn ceremony at an altar, she commits her chastity to the protection of the gods Mercury and Diana. In the next act, there is a contrasting scene in which Syphax, thwarted at first, solemnly invokes Erichtho to "infernal music." In any literal or realistic sense this is all implausible to say the least, and if it works at all, it does so in terms of the overall artifice, with its deliberate unreality, turning Sophonisba into a figure emblematic of chastity, and Syphax into a figure emblematic of lust. Their confrontation, rather than the ostensible theme of the Carthaginian wars, is, indeed, the centre of the play.

Chapman's play is in many ways similar. It is more consciously Marlovian in its presentation of Bussy as one who would arrogate to himself all authority for his action: "Let me be king myself, as man was made."[21] (II.i.197.) It also appears different from *Sophonisba* in that it is almost certainly printed from an author's manuscript and not from a copy of the play used in the theatre;[22] it has few stage directions, and these are often inadequate, and sometimes in Latin, and do not indicate theatrical practice. It is thus less easy to grasp the degree to which this play was held in check by ritual and ceremony. There are notable links with *Sophonisba*; again the grandeur of heroic figures is established not in action but by rhetorical devices, as in the use of epic simile, the bringing on of a Nuntius to describe in epic terms the duel fought by Bussy and his comrades, or the elaborate personifications of "Envy" or "Revenge" in this scene (II.i). The sense of epic grandeur is created in the language, as presumably the boys who acted the play could not display it physically, and the action, as in *Sophonisba*, really turns on the confrontation of Bussy and Tamyra, in a love which eventually destroys him. Here, too, is to be found a series of sensational effects, the Friar bringing Bussy through a vault to Tamyra, the raising of Behemoth and spirits of the underworld, and Montsurry pulling Tamyra on stage by the hair. This exactly parallels Syphax dragging on Sophonisba, but whereas Syphax merely threatens rape, Montsurry both threatens torture and carries it out, putting Tamyra on the rack or some engine of the kind, after stabbing her twice, all in full view of the audience.

[21]A similar note is struck in the presentation of the minor figure Asdrubal in *Sophonisba*, who claims, "The God of wisemen is themselves, not luck" (II.iii).
[22]See *Bussy D'Ambois*, edited by Nicholas Brooke (Revels Plays, 1964), p. lxi.

Such effects, like the use of a letter written in blood, and the Ghost of Friar Comolet, suggest a play on the same pattern as *Sophonisba*.

I do not wish to question or examine Chapman's superiority in ethical complexity, or in the quality of his verse, but at the heart of the play is a series of incidents which at first sight seem grotesquely sensational.[23] Although *Bussy D'Ambois* lacks the strong ceremonial framework of *Sophonisba*, it does have some comparable elements. Perhaps in this play the stateliness of the rhetorical grandeur of the opening and close of the play provide the main aesthetic control. This establishes the greatness of Bussy in the first two acts, and his equivocal position as amoral in spite of his talk of virtue, and returns at the end of the play, notably when Monsieur and the Guise talk "above" in choric terms about the fall of Bussy, generalizing with lofty personifications of Nature and Chance.[24] Indeed, Chapman's play, like Marston's, appears to be exploiting the boys in a new way for what they could do; they could not act out heroes, as the epic image in these plays is established by rhetoric, ceremonial, and stateliness of verse and action, but they could be used to act out what men, the adult actors, could not do. In Act IV of *Sophonisba*, the heroine challenges Syphax,

> frame unto thy lusts
> Imagination's utmost sin;

this extremity of sin or cruelty or sexual violence the boys could act out, as in the torture of Tamyra, for the artifice of the dialogue, of the boys playing heroes, prevented the horror from taking its full effect, while giving the audience a thrill. It works in its own way, allowing actual tortures, the extremes of cruelty to women, to be carried out on stage, while the audience simultaneously knew the whole thing was fantastic, a charade acted by boys. But for the

[23]Many writers on Chapman's plays have been concerned mainly, like Ennis Rees in *The Tragedies of George Chapman* (1954), with the dramatist's "ethical purpose," and have paid little attention, if any, to the dramatic and theatrical problems raised by *Bussy D'Ambois*. The outstanding essays on the play are perhaps those by E. M. Waith, comparing the Herculean figure of Bussy with Marlowe's Tamburlaine, in *The Herculean Hero* (1962); by Millar MacLure, in *George Chapman: A Critical Study* (1966), where the author argues that the absurdities of the action are "cancelled by the spirit of Bussy"; and by Nicholas Brooke who, in his edition of the play, attempts to justify the "melodrama" of the action in relation to the "philosophy" of the play, without, I think, succeeding in what is nevertheless a difficult and interesting argument.

aesthetic controls built into the play, and into the nature of the children's theatre, it might seem often grotesque. Chapman indeed courts absurdity when the Friar "ascends" as Tamyra is on the rack bleeding, and speaks as if to intervene:

> What rape of honour and religion?
> O wrack of nature. (V.i.147)

At this point he suddenly drops dead, and is said later (V.ii.59) to have died "a natural death;" in other words, he apparently dies here of shock. It is notable that in the revisions made to the play, perhaps about 1610-1612, perhaps later, the Friar is made to appear "with a sword drawn," as if to indicate rather a fight with Montsurry.[25]

Perhaps the last phase of tragedy for the boys came with Chapman's *Conspiracy* and *Tragedy of Byron* in 1607-8. In these plays Chapman wrote what *Bussy D'Ambois* is sometimes said to be, a tragedy of ideas, and turned drama into debate. This development was perhaps already implicit in the posing and taking of attitudes in *Bussy D'Ambois*, as in the set exchange of insults in 35-line speeches between Monsieur and Bussy (III.ii.336ff.). *The Tragedy of Byron* is designed to display simultaneously Byron's conviction of his own innocence and his participation in treason, or to show, in the words of Epernon, "Oh of what contraries consists a man!" (V.iii.189). Byron's "mighty merit" and "monstrous crime" (V.ii. 277) lead to a protracted death scene in Act V, in which he strikes a fine and noble attitude in accepting the equivocal "victory of death" (V.iv.261), and the play's consistent drive to this point makes it arguably one of Chapman's finest. However, it has virtually no action, and Chapman throws away his opportunities to depict "an inner struggle."[26] The clash in the play is between Byron the "natural" king, and King Henry of France; Byron glories in his self-sufficient strength, and in the conviction that

> There is no danger to a man that knows
> What life and death is; there's not any law

[24]I am indebted here to Brooke's comments on Monsieur and the Guise; see his edition, p. xlix.

[25]Brooke, *op. cit.*, p. 119, says this "probably reflects stage practice, but seems to imply death by suicide, or fighting"; if so, it reflects the stage practice of the Whitefriars company, or of the King's Men, rather than that of the boys who originally acted the play.

[26]Parrott, *The Plays and Poems of George Chapman: The Tragedies*, p. 594.

> Exceeds his knowledge; neither is it lawful
> That he should stoop to any other law.
> He goes before them, and commands them all,
> That to himself is a law rational.
>
> (*Conspiracy.* III.iii.140)

The other characters tend to fall into the background, but even the climactic encounters of Byron and the King remain static, and tend to turn to ritual, as in Act V of *The Conspiracy*, where Henry preaches at the treacherous Byron, and, as if he were a priest ministering, both cures himself of his own anger and brings himself to a sudden acceptance of Byron's professed repentance. The scene refuses to exploit the possibilities of conflict between the two men. Apart from a decorous masque in Act I of *The Tragedy of Byron*, there is little stage action or movement, and speeches tend to develop to a great length.

The later tragedies performed at the private theatres do not really belong to the story of the children's companies, for the Queen's Revels company at Whitefriars from 1610 to 1613 certainly contained some mature men among its actors; the boys had grown up, and Nathan Field, who played Bussy later for the King's Men, and may have been the first of this role, was 23 in 1610. In 1613 the company was absorbed into the adult group, the Lady Elizabeth's Men. Chapman's *The Revenge of Bussy D'Ambois*, (1610?) with its idealized stoic hero, seems to have been a flop, but it prompted Nathan Field and Chapman to revise *Bussy D'Ambois*, and their new version passed into the repertory of the King's Men, and was certainly revised as late as 1634 by them. One of the principal effects of the changes made in the revisions was to emphasize the melodrama, especially of the last act,[27] and its continuing success on the stage may be attributed in part to a change of taste or of moral atmosphere, which made acceptable at the adult theatres what only the children could present in 1604 or 1605. The stabbing of a woman and other varieties of violence between the sexes soon became almost commonplace, as in some plays of Beaumont and Fletcher, like *The Maid's Tragedy* and *Philaster*, or in the tragedies of Webster and Ford. Here again, however, the children's theatre gave the lead, and it is, of course,

---

[27]Brooke, *op. cit.*, p. lxix, traces a double motive in the revisions, "a change of scene-order for stage convenience, and accompanying changes betraying a taste for melodramatic plots."

partly due to the strength of Chapman's conception of Bussy that his play, rather than *Sophonisba*, achieved success with the adult players.

If my interpretation of the development of tragedy at the children's theatres is correct, then four phases of activity can be perhaps distinguished. The first is marked by the satirical, self-mocking inventiveness of *Antonio's Revenge* and *The Malcontent*, with perhaps *Hoffman* to be considered as well. The adult theatres appear to have seized on and developed the possibilities which these plays opened up, and in a second phase of activity after 1604, there was a new attempt at serious tragedy, exploiting sex and violence in an epic context in *Sophonisba* and *Bussy D'Ambois*. Chapman's lone effort to take this further to one logical conclusion in the Byron plays as tragedies of ideas, almost emptied of action so that they become debates, marks the third phase. The fourth, which I have hardly touched on, belongs to the period of 1610-13, when the boys, maturing into men, were to be absorbed in the adult theatre. Then plays like *The Insatiate Countess* and *Cupids Revenge* show tragedy converting itself into tragi-comedy, which was becoming the staple fare of the adult stage. In these later phases too the children's theatres seem to have given a lead in showing how sex and violence could be exploited, and in building a play out of a debate or clash of ideas. They also contributed to the establishment of tragi-comedy as a mode in the Jacobean theatre. The few tragedies of theirs that survive may not include a masterpiece, but they are remarkable for their inventiveness and sense of innovation, of something new and interesting being offered on the stage. Marston liked to say of his comedies "the life of these things consists in action," and to imply, like Chapman, that tragedies were more appropriate to be read; but it is necessary to recover a sense of the "action" of the tragedies too, if we are really to see the achievement of the children's theatres in proper perspective.

A Neglected Jones/Webb Theatre Project, Part II: A Theatrical Missing Link

D. F. ROWAN

In my paper as originally delivered at the Second Annual Inter
national Conference on Elizabethan Theatre, I offered certain sug
gestions concerning the drawings reproduced on pages 62 and
63.[1] In this published redaction I have attempted to incorporate
the preliminary conclusions presented at that time into an advanc
ing study which is a continuation and expansion of that basic
paper. Those who wish to examine the genesis of my earlier argu
ments will find them fully set forth elsewhere.[2] In my closing re
marks last summer I indicated my belief in the importance and
significance of these drawings to any future study of the Eliza
bethan theatre. I also expressed my intense awareness of the
dangers of arguing "in vacuo," at the same time hoping that future
work would answer the "vital questions of provenance, date and
identity." My hopes have not been fulfilled, for additional "hard"
evidence has not been forthcoming. Nevertheless I shall still ven
ture forth on perilous seas, my only defence being an acute con
sciousness of the dangers.

Perhaps the least perilous of questions is that of provenance; I

---

[1] I am indebted to the Provost and Fellows of Worcester College, Oxford, for
their kind permission to publish the drawings.
[2] "A Neglected Jones/Webb Theatre Project: Barber-Surgeons Hall Writ
Large," *New Theatre Magazine*, IX, No. 3 (Summer, 1969), 6-15. An exten
sive abstract of this article will appear in *Shakespeare Survey 23*, 1970.

onsider the authenticity of the drawings as almost beyond dis-
pute. Drawings 7B and 7C occur in the first volume of the Jones/
Webb collection in the Library of Worcester College, Oxford, and
here can be little doubt that they represent the designs of Inigo
Jones. As I shall demonstrate more fully later, it is clear that they
are related to the drawings of the Cockpit-in-Court (number 27 in
the same collection) and it is now certain that the design of the
Cockpit is the work of Jones. The hand which actually made the
Cockpit drawings is less certain, but recent investigation points to
John Webb. Despite similarities of design, however, the manner
and execution of the two sets of drawings are remarkably different.
Perhaps the most obvious distinction between them is in the shad-
ing; drawings 7B and 7C use ink-wash and their overall tone is
lighter and more delicate than that of the Cockpit drawings where
lines and heavy cross-hatching are used. Certainty is not possible,
but I cannot resist the negative conclusion that drawings 7B and
7C are not in the hand of Webb. The possibility that the drawings
are by Jones himself cannot be dismissed on the basis of the evidence to hand.

The compiler of the Worcester College collection associated
these two drawings with two other drawings of the "Theater of
Anatomie" of the Barber-Surgeons Company of London. As I suggested in my earlier paper, it remains possible that the distinctive
shape and proportions of the Hall of that Company may have inspired this theatre project by Jones, but, if so, I am now convinced
that Jones must have viewed the Hall some years before his later
extensive work for the Company in 1635 and 1636. The evidence
supports such an earlier date for the drawings. Their relationship
to the Cockpit design indicates that they antedate that theatre,
and the evidence of the watermarks of the paper on which the
drawings are made reinforces this supposition. Drawings 7B and
7C carry a watermark of the family illustrated by Edward Heawood (*Watermarks . . .*, Hilversum, 1950) on Plate 238. The mark
is a crowned fleur-de-lis with a pendant monogram, "WR," clearly
in the series listed by Heawood as figures 1761, 1762, 1768 and
1769. This series has a chronological range dating from 1592 to
1616. Thus, while I cannot offer positive proof for either the provenance or the date, the evidence persuades me that the drawings
are the work of the King's Surveyor, and that they probably date

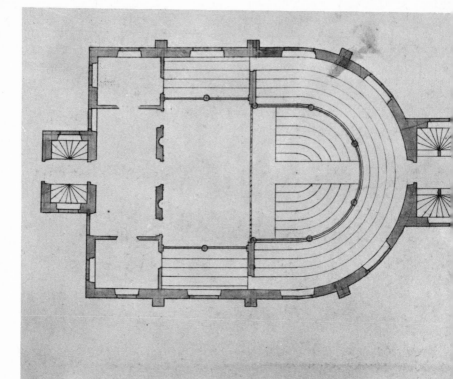

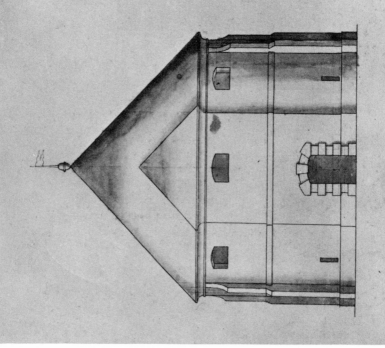

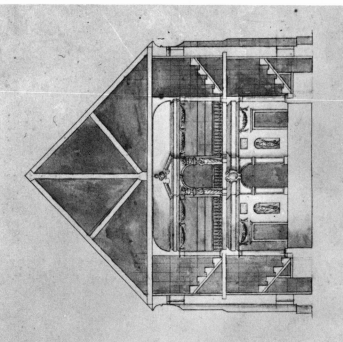

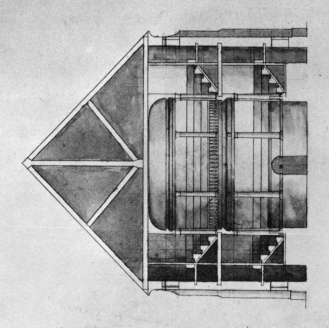

from the twenty-five-year period between the attachment of Jones to the Court (1605) and the building of the Cockpit-in-Court (1630).

The question of the identity of the pictured theatre remains the most serious problem facing the investigator. A close and detailed examination of all available evidence has failed to suggest a probable, or even a likely, candidate. Even if one were willing to accept a later date for the drawings, it would still be difficult to believe that a stage of such "conventional" design would have been considered by any of the post-Restoration theatrical entrepreneurs and for this reason I dismiss the converted tennis court and the "new" theatres of Davenant and Killigrew. For the same reason one must surely discount the repairs and reconstruction carried out at the Phoenix and Salisbury Court in the years immediately before 1660.

It is certain that the Blackfriars was a rectangular theatre, and Wright, describing the theatrical triumvirate of the early seventeenth century – the Blackfriars, the Phoenix and the Salisbury Court – in his *Historia Histrionica*, remembers that they "were all three built almost exactly alike, for Form and Bigness." It is impossible to believe that if one of these theatres had had such an unusual shape, it would not have been remarked.

Two possibilities may remain; neither very likely or capable of anything approaching proof. The first of these is the Whitefriars. G. E. Bentley writes of this obscure private playhouse that "the theatre was in the precincts of the Old Carmelite monastery, between Fleet Street and the Thames, just west of Water Lane, but its precise location in the old monastic buildings is not known."[3] It is known, however, that the theatre was in use by the Children of the Revels for some years before 1615, when the lease on the property expired, and that they were forced to seek playing space elsewhere. Perhaps a careful examination of old surveys and maps of this area would reveal a building of this peculiar shape. Although such a building might have been part of the old monastic foundation – in some ways its shape suggests a converted church – I am not too sanguine.

Perhaps a more likely candidate, but no more susceptible to proof, is the theatre known variously as Porter's Hall, Rosseter's Blackfriars and Puddle Wharf. The evidence presented by Bentley

[3]*The Jacobean and Caroline Stage* (1969), VI, 115.

(VI, 77-86) proves that a group of determined men led by one Philip Rosseter succeeded, or nearly succeeded, in building and establishing a new playhouse "within the Precinct of the Blacke ffryers neere Puddle Wharfe." This playhouse was to house the Children of the Queen's Revels – lately from the Whitefriars – newly amalgamated with the Lady Elizabeth's company, to which Prince Charles's company was later added. Some of the evidence suggests that large sums of money were spent on the property, and that two highly experienced theatrical men, Philip Henslowe and Edward Alleyn, were both associated with the project. It is clear, as well, that the theatre must have been favoured by some in high places; the King himself at one time countenanced and supported the building. It is not impossible that Inigo Jones might have undertaken the design of such a new theatre, begun with such high hopes and higher backing, but destined to founder on the ancient hostility of the City to the players.

Davenant's projected theatre of 1639 remains one final possibility. Jones and Davenant were closely associated, and the date – a decade after the Cockpit-in-Court – is not impossible. However, Davenant proposed "a Theatre or Playhouse, with necessary tireing and retireing rooms and other places convenient, containing in the whole forty yards square at the most, wherein Plays, musical entertainments, Scenes or other like Presentments, may be presented" (Bentley, VI, 305). Such an ambitious project implies a large house and not the small private theatre of our drawings.

There is thus no documentary evidence that the playhouse was ever built. Similarly, a search of such maps and surveys of seventeenth-century London as I have been able to examine offers no cartographic evidence. While such negative evidence cannot prove that such a playhouse never existed, on balance I believe that one must proceed on the assumption that this Jones/Webb theatre project was never realized, that it remains simply one further provocative design from the teeming mind of Inigo Jones.

Despite the reservations occasioned by the lack of "hard" evidence, I am driven to argue that the drawings retain their vital importance to our study of the Elizabethan theatre; that they, in fact, constitute a theatrical missing link between the public theatre of the Swan drawing and the royal theatre at Whitehall, bodied forth in the drawings of the Cockpit-in-Court. Such a position would perhaps be untenable if the drawings existed only in isolation, or

if they contradicted theories of the Elizabethan stage based on
other more solid evidence. But, in fact, the drawings lie firmly in
the line of development beginning with the medieval booth stage
and culminating in the Cockpit-in-Court. Far from offering conflicting evidence, they corroborate conclusions reached by the most
recent theoretical attempts to reconstruct the Elizabethan stage -
conclusions based on the most diverse and disparate evidence.

Recent studies of the Cockpit-in-Court have demonstrated that
this playhouse was not simply a royal toy, a côterie theatre for
elegant amateurs of the Court, but a practicable professional playhouse designed to meet the needs of the most professional of acting companies, the King's Men.[4] Such was the skill of Jones that
he succeeded in creating a superficially classical theatre elegantly
reflecting both the glory of a Renaissance prince and his own interest in neo-Vitruvian theory, while at the same time meeting the
staging requirements of the professional repertoire. The structural
limitations of the existing Cockpit suggested the curved façade of
the tiring house, and presented Jones with the opportunity of
providing the five doors and semi-circular seating arrangements
of the classical theatre. I believe that three doors would have
answered all the actors' requirements, but that they made no objection to the additional doors which satisfied the architect's classical instincts without interfering with their needs. The upper area -
for which there is absolutely no classical precedent - was essential to the performance of their plays and was, therefore, provided
by Jones. Because of the special non-commercial nature of this
royal theatre, no provision could be made, or needed to be made,
for spectators above or over the stage.

At the opposite end of a social and chronological spectrum lies
the Swan, another theatre rehabilitated by recent scholarship. It is
now generally agreed that the Swan drawing faithfully depicts a
playhouse within the main line of Elizabethan theatrical development. Basically, we find a large projecting stage without a rail with
two doors set flat in a tiring-house façade, on top of which is an
upper area for actors, spectators and musicians.

I propose that the drawings under discussion represent a theatre
which lies roughly midway - on the same social and chronological

---

[4]D. F. Rowan, "The Cockpit-in-Court," *The Elizabethan Theatre* [I], ed.
David Galloway (1969), 89-102; Glynne Wickham, "The Cockpit Reconstructed," *Shakespeare's Dramatic Heritage* (1969), pp. 151-162.

spectrum – between the Swan and the Cockpit-in-Court, and that these drawings confirm the essential features of both: a series of doors set flat in a tiring-house façade backing an unraked thrust stage, and topped by a multi-purpose upper area. I further suggest that the drawings reflect the major features of the Elizabethan *stage* as it existed in all the private playhouses. The curved auditorium, however, is a desideratum proposed by Jones, perhaps rooted in the traditional shape of the public playhouses, but nourished by the example of the classical theatres in which he was so deeply interested. This curved auditorium provides a solution to one of the central problems facing the designers of neo-Vitruvian theatres – the adaptation of the circular shape favoured by Vitruvius to the rectangular buildings available in the Courts of the Renaissance.

My belief that the drawings represent the essential features of the Elizabethan *stage* as it actually was is obliquely supported by the existence of the theatre plan found by W. G. Keith in Jones' own copy of Palladio.[5] There can be no doubt that the pressure of Jones' genius and his natural inclinations moved him toward the design of the great scenic stages which were the hallmark of the post-Restoration theatres – such a perspective stage is the centre of Jones' imaginative plan, which may well anticipate the Teatro Farnese (1618-19) at Parma. But, just as Jones' imaginative force was circumscribed in the design of the Cockpit by the physical restrictions of the existing building and the practical needs of the players, so his natural drive toward the scenic stage was held in check by the facts of the Elizabethan stage as they actually existed. It is difficult to explain in any other way the traditional and conventional stage, which the drawings depict.

Finally, I should be far less certain of my line of argument were it not for the striking independent corroboration of the main features of the drawings provided by Richard Hosley's recent theoretical reconstruction of the stage of the Second Blackfriars.[6] I am unable to follow Hosley's arguments in his assumption that the tiring house was built completely inside the hall – the 66 feet of the Hawkins' deposition[7] – nor can I regard Hosley's stepped

[5]Lily B. Campbell, *Scenes and Machines on the English Stage* . . . (1923), pp. 204-206.
[6]Richard Hosley, "A Reconstruction of the Second Blackfriars," *The Elizabethan Theatre* [I] ed. Galloway, 74-88.
[7]Irwin Smith, *Shakespeare's Blackfriars Playhouse* (1964), pp. 516ff.

galleries as either likely or proved, but it is hardly an exaggeration to say that drawing 7C could serve as an illustration for his provocative theoretical study. There is agreement on a number of important points: a gallery over the stage for both actors and spectators; a stage without a rail running across the width of the playhouse; seats for spectators along the side of a stage with almost precisely an 8:5 ratio; and a flat tiring-house façade with three doors. This remarkable agreement of the two sets of evidence, from totally independent sources, must support my contention that the drawings are closely related to the actual stage of the Elizabethan theatre.

Let us for the moment turn aside from speculation to examine the drawings themselves. If we accept the scales as representing 5 feet and one foot, we have a small, unusually shaped "private" playhouse with a maximum interior width of 37 feet and a length of 52 feet. A fine sense of proportion places the front edge of the 4-foot-high stage precisely at the midpoint – 26 feet from the back wall of a tiring house just slightly over 10 feet in depth and stretching the width of the theatre. On each side of the stage, galleries measuring 6 feet, 9 inches leave a stage 23 feet, 6 inches wide, and 15 feet deep. The front wall of the tiring house is broken by an arched central door 8 feet high and 4 feet wide, and flanked on either side by rectangular doors 6 feet high, and 2 feet, 6 inches wide. From the floor of the pit to the curved ceiling is a distance of 26 feet, 9 inches. In this height the architect has placed two galleries, the first of which rises 11 feet above the level of the stage, and the second, an additional 7 feet. These galleries are broken at the midpoint of the playhouse: both the upper and lower galleries of the "house end" of the building have four degrees and space for a walkway behind the last row. These galleries are approximately 7 feet, 6 inches in depth. The lower galleries of the "stage end" appear to end against the tiring-house wall, and also have four degrees but no walkway behind. The upper galleries at this end also have four degrees and no walkway, and may (the drawing is not clear on this point) continue unbroken around the upper stage corner. There are, however, only three degrees of seats above the stage and they are interrupted by a classically ornamented "window" 4 feet wide. In the pit are oval degrees gracefully reflecting the curve of the playhouse wall. Divided by a central gangway,

hey probably rise to the 4-foot level of both the stage and the floor
of the first gallery.

Despite the fact that this is clearly a private playhouse – small,
roofed, with seats in the orchestra – it is remarkable how the stage
and seating arrangements reflect the public playhouses as we conceive them to have been. Perhaps it is no more than coincidence,
but the location of the front line of the stage proceeding along the
centre line of the playhouse cannot fail to recall the stage of the
Fortune which is "to extend to the middle of the yard of the said
house." The seats along the sides of the stage, the places for spec-
ators in the upper area back of the stage, the rising sweep of the
enclosing circular galleries, must have recreated in this private
house that sense of intimacy, of audience pressure, which must
have been so characteristic of the great public theatres. How fam-
liar it must all have seemed to the actors!

As noted earlier, the floor of the lower gallery is approximately
level with the floor of the stage, and this enables the architect to
avoid the stepped galleries which seem to me one of the questionable conclusions of Hosley's reconstruction. The solution proposed
in these drawings is architecturally sounder, and my own feeling
is that the builder of the Blackfriars might well have chosen to
place the floor of the first gallery at stage level and to reduce the
height of his galleries to achieve simplicity of construction. However, as the architect of our playhouse was content with two galleries within an overall height of slightly over 26 feet, his problems
were not as severe as those of an architect who may have attempted
three galleries within 32 feet. Because of the fact that in this unknown theatre the floor of the galleries is above the floor of the pit,
I suggest that the degrees shown in drawing 7B might well have
sloped up to this 4-foot height at the back of the pit. Unfortunately,
the elevation shown on 7C is defective, and the degrees in the pit
are not shown.

Since the publication of the Swan drawing in 1888, the vexing
question of the use of the "upper area," over or above the stage, has
exercised scholars. Most recently, Herbert Berry in his carefully
documented paper, "The Playhouse in the Boar's Head Inn, White-
chapel,"[8] has offered much interesting evidence about the use of
the area in that theatre. At the centre of a long and involved law-

The Elizabethan Theatre [I], ed. Galloway, 45-73.

suit rests the question of who should have the profits from th "gallaries over the stage." One document uses the phrase six time and there can be no doubt that the area was highly prized b spectators at the Boar's Head. At the same time evidence for th use of an upper acting area fills the plays of every professiona company, of every theatre, both public and private, for over half : hundred years. Because of the special nature of the Cockpit-in Court there was no provision for spectators over the stage, but a upper acting area was provided. I have recently completed a de tailed study of over twenty plays produced at the Cockpit betwee 1630 and 1638, and of these plays at least eight demand the use o the upper area. Surely the answer to this question is found in : multi-purpose upper area, used by spectators, actors or musician as circumstance permitted or occasion demanded. Such an "uppe area" is found in 7C where there is clearly a small ornamente "window" or upper stage and, just as clearly, degrees for spectator That the horizontal lines along the back of the upper area over th stage are not mere remnants of the draughtsman's guide lines i proved by the concession to the area's difficult sight lines; there ar only three tiers of seats. One must note as well the care with whic the drawing shows that the seats do not carry through behind th "window."

Although the dimensions of the pictured theatre are small, it capacity is surprising. Ignoring "the oblique caves and wedges c the house" and allowing 2 linear feet for each spectator, I estimat that it could easily seat 500 people, only a few less than the lates estimate of the capacity of the Second Blackfriars.[9] This seemingl large capacity is made possible by considerable vertical crowding that is by the placing of four degrees or rows of seats within th relatively shallow depth of the galleries: 6 foot, 8 inches along th stage and 7 feet, 6 inches in the auditorium. This gives a shar vertical rise to the seats and good sight lines, but leaves little spac for knees. I have tried to be conservative in my estimate which is a follows: 120 in the pit, 240 in the upper and lower "house" gallerie 112 in the "stage" galleries, and 24 over the stage, for a total of 49(

The drawings are elegantly finished – in fact they suggest "sho drawings" of some sort – but they present a number of "problems which presumably would have had to be resolved before actua construction could begin. The most serious is a seemingly insolubl

[9]Irwin Smith, *op. cit.*, p. 297.

confusion of levels in the plan drawing on 7B. The "stage end" of the plan must be at ground level (there is no indication of the second story "window" or the seats for the spectators over the stage), but since the entrance corridor to the pit is cut off from the exterior door, the "house end" must show the upper gallery. The two exits, right and left, from the tiring house immediately back of the stage appear curiously unfinished, and the stage elevation on 7C does not show the doors at the back of the lower stage galleries which are indicated on the plan view. Entrance to the stage galleries could have been through these doors from the tiring house, or from the walkways at the back of the "house galleries." Other galleries present problems of access which are not readily solved in the drawings. The oval degrees of 7B do not appear in the elevation on 7C. No doors are shown in any of the apertures, either on the stage or in the playhouse proper. What appears to be a wicket in what might be taken as a door in the elevation of the "house end" on 7C is merely a blot. The drawings are thus of small help in settling the question as to the existence of doors or curtains or both on the Elizabethan stage.

These drawings also fail to present three features which we know from other evidence to have existed. There is no indication of a trapdoor, but there can be no doubt that there was one. No trap is shown in either the Swan or the Cockpit drawing, but the evidence of the plays themselves is certain on this point. The drawings fail to delineate, as well, the place for flying machinery, although the evidence of the plays is once again incontrovertible. The sturdy rafters shown in 7C could have supported the necessary gear, although the central tie beam might have presented some difficulties. Finally, there is no provision for artificial lighting. A number of fairly large windows appear on both plane and elevation views, but there is little doubt that artificial lighting was a usual feature of the private theatre. The only explanation for these lapses and the earlier noted inconsistencies is that the drawings are not fully worked out – further evidence that the playhouse was never built.

Perhaps the most persuasive evidence about the provenance of these drawings is the most subjective. If one compares the elevation of the "stage end" of the playhouse on drawing 7C with the elevation of the Cockpit-in-Court, the overall impression that the stages are identical is well nigh overwhelming. The two additional doors of the Cockpit are masked in the curve of the side walls, and the

remarkable similarity of the two tiring-house façades is strikingly
revealed. The similar proportions and relationships of all features
the rounded central doors with the smaller square flanking doors
the decorative medallions and plaques, the classical pediments
above the upper windows – in short the tragic scene "delineated
with columns, pediments, statues, and other objects suited to
Kings" – combine to produce the irresistible impression that both
stages are the work of a single architect, the incomparable Inigo
Jones. As in the Cockpit, there can be no question of the use of the
central "royal door" as anything more than a "discovery space."
Apart from the differences in the shapes of the stages (the unusual
shape of the Cockpit stage was forced on Jones by the existing
structure), and the number of doors – a point which we have already
considered – the single discrepancy is the presence of a stage railing
in the Cockpit. Interestingly, recent scholarship based on the works
accounts of the Restoration period suggests that the railings at the
Cockpit were a Restoration addition. They are not mentioned in
the earlier works accounts.

Finally, one might note the distinctive oblique seating in the pits
of both theatres. I suggest that Jones has adapted the earlier seating
plan mooted in these drawings to the special needs of a royal
theatre, and solved the nasty seating problem of the central corner
seats by simply doing away with them in the Cockpit. On balance
then, the evidence of the more sophisticated seating plan of the
Cockpit, combined with its more elaborately developed classical
façade and reinforced by the fact that the watermarks on the
drawings have a known upper limit of 1616, leads me to the inescapable conclusion that these drawings represent a theatre project
of Inigo Jones conceived sometime before the building of the
Cockpit in 1630.

Questionable as some of my individual assumptions may be, I am
emboldened by an emerging pattern of consistency to reiterate that
these drawings constitute a theatrical missing link between the
Swan and the Cockpit-in-Court, between the public "professional"
theatre and the royal "professional" theatre. Whether the drawings
are by Inigo Jones or not, or whether they antedate or postdate the
Cockpit are important questions, but, to a degree, irrelevant. So
too, is the question as to whether the theatre was or was not actually
built. Whatever may be the answers to these questions the drawings remain. There can be no doubt that they represent a real or

proposed private "professional" theatre, and close the gap between the public and royal stages of which we have direct visual evidence. With this final piece of visual evidence set in place the mosaic may be complete. Is it unreasonable to see the stage from 1576 to 1642 as a continuum, a fabric woven of the unbroken threads of stage conditions, acting conventions, and audience expectation when they entered a playhouse: they expected and saw an unraked thrust stage without a rail, surrounded on three sides by spectators, sometimes on and sometimes off the stage; a tiring-house façade with two or three doors, perhaps the central one larger, but not large enough for anything more than a brief discovery; and a multi-purpose upper area over the stage used by actors and spectators and musicians. Public, private and royal stages were all of a piece – the actors and audience at home in each.

The Elizabethan Theatre
and the Inductive Method

J. A. LAVIN

In an article in the 1969 volume of *Studies in Bibliography*, D. F. McKenzie shows that the inductive method has been widely used by analytical bibliographers, who have extracted general laws from particular instances.[1] Despite the fact that they work with the evidence of real books, the scientific flavour of bibliographers' conclusions about early printing practices and so-called typical Elizabethan printers is spurious, because no finite number of particular instances can ever prove a general law. Certain bibliographical facts may suggest a hypothesis that explains them, but their existence does not prove the hypothesis correct. For this reason, says McKenzie, we should work, not inductively, but deductively, first collecting all the available information about the working arrangements of early printing houses, which were both variable and complex, and then establishing hypotheses on the basis of what was demonstrably possible. The hypotheses should then be tested against the facts of particular cases. Such hypotheses, arrived at deductively, are not necessarily correct, but are more likely to be so than those established inductively.

McKenzie demonstrates this by examining various widely accepted hypotheses of analytical bibliography in the light of his intimate knowledge of the real printing-house practices of the early Cambridge University Press, supplemented by the records of Plantin, Bowyer, Strahan, and the Societé Typographique de Neuchâtel.

[1]D. F. McKenzie, "Printers of the Mind: Some Notes on Bibliographical Theories and Printing-House Practices," *Studies in Bibliography*, XXII (1969), 1-75.

These negate the assumption that hand-press printers worked largely on one book at a time and reveal that the normal practice for even small two-press shops, as the records show, was to have ten or twelve titles in production concurrently. The production patterns were consequently very complex, and took into account the huge disparity in the output of various employees. Simple conclusions about numbers of copies in an edition, or about production time, deriving from assumptions about the necessary balance between composition and press-work, are now shown not to correspond to the facts of real printing.

As an illustration, McKenzie applies the inductive method, usually employed in such cases, to an investigation of the 1713 edition of Newton's *Principia*, and then goes on to show that his plausible conclusions are completely at variance with the actual printing methods that were used in the book's production. He thus demolishes many of the elaborate theories that have been erected on analyses of skeleton formes.

In dealing similarly with various other accepted bibliographical theories McKenzie concludes time and again that the primary documentation shows the actual working of real printing houses to have been complex and variable, and much "scientific" bibliography of the last thirty years or so to have been simplistic and mistaken.

Similar criticism may be levelled at the conclusions of many historians of the Elizabethan theatre, an area where the inductive method is also widely used. In this connection, the comments made thirty years ago by George Reynolds in his Introduction to *The Staging of Elizabethan Plays at the Red Bull Theater* (1940), are still valid:

> There have also been too many generalizations from a few instances; too many uncontrolled suppositions of what might have been, without any ascertained facts of Elizabethan procedure to support them. . . . In short, many of our present conclusions rest on unsound foundations which demand re-examination. (p. 2).

For years the habit of extracting general laws from particular instances has bedevilled the study of the physical structure of Elizabethan playhouses, and where this has been combined with unsupported assumptions about particular physical features, it has given rise to such laws as the existence of the inner stage and all its interpretive consequences.[2] It has taken the persistent efforts of Richard Hosley and other scholars such as Herbert Berry and D. F. Rowan to undermine this well-established myth, and the battle is perhaps not yet finally won.[3]

But a word of caution is necessary here. The inductive method is so deeply engrained as a scholarly habit that even these gentlemen should be reminded of its central flaw. Because one sees only white swans, or DeWitt Swans, does not necessarily mean that there are, or were, no black swans, or, if you like, non-DeWitt Swans. One sees the inductive method lurking, for instance, beneath Professor Hosley's defence of the Swan drawing as "not only typical of Elizabethan public playhouses but also capable of accommodating the production of nearly all extant Elizabethan plays"[4] – a statement which, at the least, invites us to extrapolate from the Swan, and which strongly implies that other Elizabethan theatres were very similar, if not actually identical. We are left to speculate on the structures necessary for those plays that could not be accommodated by the stage in the Swan drawing, and on the relevance of that drawing to the reconstruction of private playhouse stages. One answer is offered by the Cockpit-in-Court drawings, which provide the five-entry stage apparently demanded by such plays as *The Dutch Courtesan* and *Eastward Ho!*[5]

More particularly, the commonly used technique of collecting and examining stage directions from the plays of one company or playhouse, in order to establish the existence of certain physical

[2]On the way in which assumptions and preconceptions have affected reconstructions of Elizabethan and Jacobean playhouses, see C. Walter Hodges, "The Lantern of Taste," *Shakespeare Survey 12* (1959), 8-14; Richard Hosley, "The Origins of the So-called Elizabethan Multiple Stage," *Tulane Drama Review*, XII (1968), 28-50; A. H. Scouten, "Some Assumptions Behind Accounts of the Elizabethan Stage," in John W. Ehrstine *et al, On Stage and Off: Eight Essays in English Literature* (Washington State University Press, 1968), pp. 4-11.

[3]See Richard Hosley, "The Discovery Space in Shakespeare's Globe," *Shakespeare Survey 12* (1959), 35-46; Herbert Berry, "The Stage and Boxes at Blackfriars," *Studies in Philology*, LXIII (1966), 163-186; Glynne Wickham, "The Cockpit Reconstructed," *New Theatre Magazine*, VII (1967), 26-36; D. F. Rowan, "The Swan Revisted," *Research Opportunities in Renaissance Drama*, X (1967), 33-47.

[4]"The Origins of the So-called Elizabethan Multiple Stage," p. 28.

[5]See Wickham, "The Cockpit Reconstructed;" and D. F. Rowan, "The Cockpit-in-Court," *The Elizabethan Theatre* [I], ed. David Galloway (Toronto, 1969), pp. 89-102; and cf. Robert M. Wren, "The Five-Entry Stage at Blackfriars," *Theatre Research*, VIII (1967), 130-38.

features in that playhouse, must be subjected to the closest scrutiny. The dangers of the method are well exemplified by the half-timbered, inner-stage reconstruction provided by Irwin Smith in *Shakespeare's Blackfriars Playhouse,* which in Herbert Berry's view perpetuates Wallace's arrangement of the stage and boxes and adds wholesale the features of J. C. Adams's Globe. Robert M. Wren points to other failings in Smith's basic methodology which are especially pertinent here: Smith assumes that the second Blackfriars remained unchanged for forty-two years, that any part of the repertoire can be used as evidence of staging for the whole period, and that the stage was similar to the Globe's, though the latter has not yet been precisely defined. He takes the plays stage-direction by stage-direction and scene by scene, and the end result is a "handsome drawing . . . hardly a detail of which is trustworthy."[6] That it is still necessary to point out how ludicrous such proceedings are is indicated by the fact that his book was published as recently as 1964.

The history of the Admiral's Men at once makes clear some of the difficulties inherent in using stage directions to establish the physical features of a particular playhouse or, indeed, in establishing a company's canon. To begin with, the assumption that the phrase "Admiral's Men" precisely defines a particular group of players is no more valid than the assumption that the second Blackfriars remained unchanged for forty-two years. Does it refer to the Howard's company of 1576-78, or the Admiral's Men of 1585-89, who may in fact have been the first Earl of Worcester's company renamed, and have had no connection with the first troupe? In any case, in 1585 the Admiral's were playing jointly with the Chamberlain's Men at Leicester and at Court. Whose plays were they performing? Between 1590 and 1594 the Admiral's were merged with Strange's, if not absorbed by them; to whose canon belong the plays performed in those years? By a reverse process the Admiral's Men largely absorbed Pembroke's in 1597, following *The Isle of Dogs,* and in 1600, having been the Rose company since 1591, became the permanent residents of the Fortune. But it is no more accurate to label them the Rose troupe or the Fortune troupe than it is to call them the Admiral's Men, for they also played at the Theatre and at Newington Butts, not to mention their Court and provincial appearances. It is perhaps best to think of them as

[6]Robert M. Wren, review in *Philological Quarterly,* XLV (1966), 165-68.

Henslowe's Men (he refers to them at least once as "my company"), although that invites confusion with other companies – Strange's, the Queen's, Sussex's – with whom Henslowe also had dealings. This is not a petty matter of mere nomenclature; it illustrates the fact that, given the constant shifting of personnel and the consequently fluid nature of the troupes, even the name of the company is not particularly meaningful.

It is therefore hardly more meaningful to ask, for any one of a number of ordinary scholarly purposes, whether a play is an Admiral's Men play, unless the question is more narrowly defined than it usually is. A preferable form would be: "Was this play acted on some occasion by a troupe then calling itself the Admiral's Men?" This allows for the complicated and dubious provenance of many plays known to have been in the Admiral's Men stock, though it begs the questions of origin and actual ownership. Shifting allegiances, temporary alliances, and the buying of old plays at various times all contributed to the book inventory of the Admiral's Men, although other plays in the company's regular repertory may well have been owned, not by the company, but by Henslowe (as with *Friar Bacon*), or by individual actors such as Alleyn, who acquired the books and properties of the pre-1590 men. However, an affirmative answer to the re-phrased question does not guarantee that a play performed by the Admiral's Men was in fact an Admiral's Men play, for there were joint performances with Hunsdon's in 1585, a four-year amalgamation with Strange's from 1590-94, and ten joint performances with the new Chamberlain's Men in 1594, including the Chamberlain's plays *Titus Andronicus*, *Hamlet*, *Hester and Ahasuerus*, and *The Taming of a Shrew*. And after the *Isle of Dogs* fiasco in 1597, but even before the Admiral's finally absorbed Pembroke's Men, they were performing some of the latter's plays.

The implications of these facts need to be considered, but before leaving the matter of nomenclature it may be mentioned that the term "children's companies" has also given rise to mistaken assumptions which have had literary-critical consequences. It will be remembered that Marston's plays were written to be performed by children's companies, and as it is now fashionable to point to his absurdism, and to compare him with Ionesco, Brecht, Beckett and Weiss, critics such as Caputi, Foakes and Hunter have naturally concerned themselves with the effect that the youthfulness of the actors must have had on the impact of his plays. In order to appreciate *Antonio and Mellida* and *Antonio's Revenge*, says Professor Foakes, "we need to bear in mind that they were written to be acted by children, boys with piping voices from the choir school of St. Paul's Cathedral."[7] But the words "boys" and "children" are themselves misleading, conjuring up images of cherubic toddlers or perhaps of eight- and nine-year-olds, instead of adolescents. It is true that Solomon Pavy, famous for his playing of old men's roles, was "scarce thirteen" when he died in 1603, but Nathan Field, mentioned in the actor-lists of *Epicoene* (1609) and *The Coxcomb* (1612), would have been twenty-two on the first night of *Epicoene*, and was already the author of *A Woman Is a Weathercock*, given at Court the same Christmas. He did not in fact join an adult company until about 1616, aged almost thirty. An equally interesting example is William Barkstead who, when he left the Children of the Queen's Revels for Lady Elizabeth's Men in 1611, was the author of the poem *Myrrha* (published in 1607), and had completed Marston's *The Insatiate Countess*, left behind on Marston's departure for clerical life in 1608. That boys whose voices had broken were retained in children's companies may also be inferred from a report of about 1602 that the Dowager Countess of Leicester had married "one of the playing boyes of the chappell."[8] The traditional concept of shrill and piping boy players must be adjusted to accommodate these facts;[9] nor should we forget the use of boys for women's roles, many of them of considerable length and complexity, by the adult troupes.

This is not to deny the existence of the "rascally tits . . . wrens or pismires" of the Induction to *Cynthia's Revels*, for although some of the boys stayed with the companies and naturally grew older, the complaint of Henry Clifton over the impressment of his son in 1600, and the commissions granted to Nathaniel Giles in 1604 and 1606 indicate that the latter was continuously recruiting. It is clear that, a few years after the revival of the children's companies in 1600, their personnel included boys, youths, and young men.

It should be added, as a further example of misleading nomen-

---

[7] R. A. Foakes, "Shakespeare's Later Tragedies," in *Shakespeare 1564-1964*, ed. Edward A. Bloom (Providence, 1964), p. 95.
[8] E. K. Chambers, *The Elizabethan Stage*, II, 48.
[9] The Children of the Queen's Revels Commission, 13 September 1604, contains a provision for the further education of boys whose voices had changed; *Malone Society Collections*, I, 359; see also Keysar's complaint (*Elizabethan Stage*, II, 57).

clature, that the private playhouses in which they performed were not private, but places of public resort, and that statements about their repertoires, acting styles and audiences are consequently often incorrect. Alfred Harbage, in *Shakespeare and the Rival Traditions* (1952), argues that there were "two distinct theatrical traditions in England, signalized by two distinct kinds of theatre," the public and private, which, he claims, had different repertories, mainly satiric comedy at the private theatres, but "romantic, idealistic, positive, and often patriotic and religious" plays at the public theatres. In a variant of the inductive method, whereby one first confuses cause and effect and then argues from a particular effect to establish a general law, Harbage points out that the private houses were in physical character designed to be exclusive; that they were therefore small; that they were completely under cover, and used artificial light; that to accommodate the gallants of the day they were located within easy reach of the Inns of Court; and that to discourage attendance by playgoers of the common sort they charged sixpence to one-and-sixpence, as opposed to one, two, or three pence at the public houses.[10]

To this one may reply that whether one accepts, in the case of the second Blackfriars, for instance, the seating figures of Harbage (less than 900), Hosley (720), or Smith (516), as compared to the Swan and Fortune capacities of 2,000 and 2,500 spectators, the fact remains that the size of the theatre was predetermined by the dimensions of the upper frater. It was not therefore small because it was designed to be exclusive, but was exclusive because the available room was small. Artificial light had to be used, because the theatre was roofed and the wooden galleries effectively blocked out most of the window light. Nor was the Blackfriars located within easy reach of the Inns of Court in order to accommodate the gallants of the day; when the Dominicans erected their buildings in 1275 it is unlikely that they had this convenience in mind. It was a combination of happy accidents that the Blackfriars precinct had taken on the character of a liberty, which it retained until 1608; that Sir Thomas Cawarden, the first Master of the Revels, had started the buildings' theatrical connection by leasing them for the Revels Office before he was given them in 1550 because of their proximity to the royal wardrobe; that Farrant's Children of the Chapel had used the premises as a theatre since 1576, and that the

[10]*Rival Traditions*, pp. 43-45.

success of Burbage's Theatre in Shoreditch was threatened by the expiry of the lease in 1597 at a time when the old Parliament Chamber was available. While the high prices charged produced a degree of exclusiveness, they were occasioned by the simple economics of limited accommodation, the constant threat of closure, and the determination of Richard and Cuthbert Burbage to make their father's costly investment show a profit.

The whirligig of time, whose evolutionary effects render it necessary to specify which of several Admiral's Men troupes we may be discussing, did not allow audience tastes, or the nature of the drama itself, to remain unchanged. Within even narrower temporal limits than are provided by a comparison of Marlowe with Beaumont and Fletcher, or early and late Shakespeare, the process can be observed. The old plays produced early in the revival of the children's companies were dismissed by Jonson and Marston as "the umbrae, or ghosts of some three or foure playes, departed a dozen yeeres since," as "mouldy fopperies of stale Poetry, / ... drie mustie Fictions" and as "mustie fopperies of antiquittie," pointing to the distance between the dramatic fashions of 1600 and those of Lyly's time. It is a commonplace of theatrical history that in the 1590s public taste changed quickly, and it can hardly be doubted that at the end of the sixteenth century there was a concomitant development in methods of acting; Bottom's demonstration of "Ercles' vein" and Falstaff's of "King Cambyses' vein" mock an acting style probably not much earlier, but different and cruder than that then in vogue. It would, therefore, be astonishing indeed if the Elector Palatine's Men were still employing in the 1620s the same acting techniques as their distant predecessors, the Howard's Men of 1576.

Bertram Joseph, however, makes a much grosser assumption than this in his book *Elizabethan Acting* (1951), which is an example of the inductive method at its worst. Whether he is right or wrong about a formal versus a naturalistic acting style is not here at issue, but his failure to define any of his terms is. The book's title might suggest temporal limits of 1558 to 1603, but it quickly becomes apparent that Professor Joseph considers the word "Elizabethan" to be interchangeable with "Renaissance." Quoting Richard Flecknoe's description of the ideal actor from his *Aenigmaticall Characters* of 1665 hardly enlightens us about Kempe, Tarlton or Burbage, and leaning heavily, as he does throughout the book, on John

J. A. Lavin

Bulwer's 1644 treatises on the use of the hand, arm and fingers in rhetorical delivery is analogous to quoting from an elocutionary treatise published in 1944 in order to illustrate what Sir Henry Irving did at the Lyceum in 1880. However interesting the illustrations in Bulwer may be, it is preposterous to derive from them a general law about acting in England in the sixteenth and seventeenth centuries. When it is asserted by Professor Joseph on his first page that "whoever knows to-day exactly what was taught to the renaissance orator cannot be far from knowing at the same time what was done by the actor on the Elizabethan stage," we must necessarily ask, "What actor, what stage, and when?"; for the phrase "the actor on the Elizabethan stage" subsumes the pageant-waggon guild performers of the miracle cycles, which survived to the end of the sixteenth century; the royal interluders; the grammar school and university actors of academic plays; the small travelling troupes which acted Moralities and Interludes in great halls; the early and later children's companies of the private theatres; and London companies such as the Admiral's Men, who acted in inn-yards, town halls, royal palaces, college halls, private dwellings, the Inns of Court, and various permanent playhouses ranging from the Theatre in 1576 to the Fortune in the 1620s.

A similar denial of the complexity, variety and flexibility of Elizabethan dramatic activity lies at the centre of T. W. Baldwin's *Organization and Personnel of the Shakespearean Company* (1927) which, despite its plethora of detail, offers a basically schematic and simplistic view of the Chamberlain's–King's Men. Professor Baldwin's approach is not unlike that of a hand-press compositor who, as you may recall, sets his material upside-down and reads it backwards. In a virtuoso demonstration of the inductive method he starts with actor lists in the Beaumont and Fletcher second folio of 1679, and with the help of five separately published plays in which parts are assigned to particular actors, argues that "each actor had a definite line" of character types in which he specialized, that "each play was so written as to contain a representative of the line of each principal actor," and that

> the play was regularly fitted to the company, not the company to the play. It ought therefore to be possible to trace these established "lines" backward, in the plays with unassigned lists, and so to trace out the "line" of each actor, together with the majority of characters in each "line" (p. 197).

82

This, inductively, he proceeds to do, first back to 1610 and ultimately to 1592, on the assumption that all the heroic young lovers' roles played by the leading actor Taylor had earlier been played by Burbage, whom he succeeded in 1619, and that the same method is valid even for minor characters. Baldwin is thus able to conclude that "Shakespeare cut his play to fit the actors of his company even in the details of age and physical appearance" (p. 282). This must have made things somewhat difficult as young men gradually metamorphosed into old men, and probably occasioned some awkwardness in the assignment of parts when the Chamberlain's played jointly with the Admiral's in 1594. In his excellent book *Shakespeare at the Globe* (1962), Bernard Beckerman has dealt sensibly, charitably, briefly and convincingly with Baldwin's arguments, pointing out that "any general tendency to specialize in [comedy or tragedy] is unlikely in view of the alternation of plays, some of which call for almost all comedians, others for almost all tragedians" (p. 135), and that "the host of different roles which a single actor was called upon to play could not have been shaped to one personality" (p. 136). Baldwin himself assigns the roles of Hamlet, Richard III, Othello, Lear, Claudio in *Much Ado*, Ford in *Merry Wives*, and Bertram in *All's Well* to Burbage. It is clear that these very different parts were not built around the personal traits of one actor.

One might add that David Bevington, in *Mankind to Marlowe* (1962), has drawn attention to the importance and longevity of the theatrical practice of doubling roles, and though one may occasionally quibble with his arithmetic, he has shown that at least in the period with which he deals, when one man in his time indeed played many parts, often in a single play, versatility and not specialization was the actor's prime requirement. The evidence points to this theatrical tradition having continued.[11]

Henslowe's *Diary* shows not only that it was common for individual actors to move to and from the Admiral's Men and other companies, but that the companies themselves played jointly, shared each other's repertory, bought each other's plays, and variously acted those owned by Alleyn or Henslowe – all extremely difficult to do if Baldwin's rigid scheme had been in effect. It is also

[1]See W. A. Ringler, "The Number of Actors in Shakespeare's Early Plays," *The Seventeenth-Century Stage*, ed. G. E. Bentley (Chicago, 1968), pp. 10-34.

relevant here to remember the contemporary gossip which represents Greene as selling *Orlando Furioso* first to the Queen's and
then to the Admiral's. And even though the new bibliography has
only relatively recently, and very properly, taught us to revere the
most miniscule details of surviving texts, it must also be said that
play texts themselves were no more in a state of stasis than any
other aspect of the theatrical enterprise. Henslowe's *Diary* shows
that old Admiral's Men plays were revised as well as revived: £6
to Dekker in 1599-1600 for a large-scale revision of *Fortunatus*; £2
the next year for "alterynge of" *Phaeton* for the Court; £2 to Jonson
in 1601 and another £2 in 1602 for his "adicyons for Jeronymo";
£4 to Bird and Rowley in 1602-3 for additions to *Dr. Faustus*; a
payment to Dekker for alterations to *Tasso's Melancholy*, and to
Middleton for a prologue and epilogue for *Friar Bacon*. Similarly
Chettle was paid £1 in 1598 for "mending" *Robin Hood*, and not
only were old plays bought from individuals and other companies
but plays commissioned for the Admiral's Men and left unfinished
were sometimes later finished for other companies, as with Dekker's
A Medicine for a Curst Wife, transferred to Worcester's Men.

These instances not only demonstrate the various companies
capacity for dealing with almost any play that was put into their
hands, but also remind us of the dramaturgic reality behind the
received text that has been sanctified by analytical bibliography.
As with any play today, the author's script would have been cut,
patched, and reworked in rehearsal, if not at those first tavern
readings recorded by Henslowe; the modern conflated text of
Hamlet, for example, is a nonce-text, almost certainly never acted
in Shakespeare's own day. Later alterations would sometimes be
necessary to accommodate changes in a company's personnel,
probably explaining, for instance, why Viola's songs are assigned
to Feste in the folio text of *Twelfth Night*. And inevitably, as actors
grew older, they would undertake different kinds of roles from
those played in youth, and would be superseded in parts they had
created. The process of revision, alteration, adaptation, and therefore evolution, of the script must have varied enormously from play
to play, as both the bibliographical and external evidence shows,
and although this stratification or onion-skin view of the text has
been overstated by John Dover Wilson in the *New Cambridge
Shakespeare*, it does reflect the prevailing realities.

Finally, one last complexity must be touched on briefly – the question of dramatic authorship itself. Generations of scholars have applied their energy and ingenuity to the various aspects of this problem, invariably employing permutations of the inductive method in the hope of assigning anonymous plays to specific authors, or of unravelling the strands of joint authorship woven by Henslowe's hacks and others. One example will suffice: the almost forgotten disintegrator J. M. Robertson, whose *Problem of Hamlet* (1919) provided the basis for T. S. Eliot's famous essay on *Hamlet* as an artistic failure, "raises aloft the banner of science; again and again he insists upon the inductive nature of his method," according to Professor Schoenbaum. Fortunately, the matter need not be gone into here, for Schoenbaum in his *Internal Evidence and Elizabethan Dramatic Authorship* (1966), has dealt fully with the methods and largely fruitless results of these quests, and if the purge he has given the gentlemen concerned is somewhat milder than that administered to Crispinus-Marston in Jonson's *Poetaster*, it nevertheless results in their vomiting up the vocabulary of confidence, in particular such words as "definitive," "certain," "vindicate," "conclusive," "infallible," "unquestionably." The last paragraph of his book is worth quoting here:

As things stand, however, many popular assumptions and facile generalizations about the nature of Elizabethan dramatic collaboration have no secure foundation in external fact, but rest instead on undemonstrated theories or on internal evidence garnered in cheerful violation of the elementary methods I have outlined in part three of this study.

It may not be necessary to conclude, as D. F. McKenzie does after surveying bibliographical theories and printing-house practices, that "wherever full primary evidence has become available it has revealed a geometry of such complexity that even an expert in cybernetics, primed with all the facts, would have little chance of discerning it" (p. 60), but it is as true of theatrical history as of bibliography that "multiple and ingenious hypotheses . . . have been allowed to harden into 'truth'" (p. 61), and that "insisting on the rigorous testing of hypotheses, and the prime method of falsification – adducing contrary particulars – would impose a sound curb on premature generalizations" (p. 61). It is difficult to disagree with McKenzie's stress on the supreme importance of primary evidence and on the danger, in using the inductive method, of erroneous inference. As a last example, the supposition, arrived at inductively, that Shakespeare altered his style expressly to fit the Blackfriars stage[12] is a general statement which is immediately damaged by the contrary fact that after the second Blackfriars became available his company used it for winter seasons from October to May, returning to the Globe from May to October.[13]

Attempts to generalize about Elizabethan theatres, acting, dramatic companies and theatrical texts are at the best naive, and at the worst positively misleading. The facets of the Elizabethan theatrical world were multifarious, and one might justifiably apply to that world the lines from Louis MacNiece's poem "Snow":

> World is crazier and more of it than we think,
> Incorrigibly plural.

---

[12]G. E. Bentley, "Shakespeare and the Blackfriars Theatre," *Shakespear Survey* 1 (1948), 38-50; A. M. Nagler, *Shakespeare's Stage* (1958), p. 102 thinks performances at the Blackfriars differed little from those at the Globe
[13]The longer version of this paper delivered at the Waterloo Conference wa entitled "The Admiral's Men and the Inductive Method." A much truncate and amended version was read at the Pacific Northwest Renaissance Confer ence in Seattle, March, 1970.

Nature and Decorum
in the Theory of
Elizabethan Acting

LISE-LONE MARKER*

Scholars have endeavoured to describe and evaluate the Shake-spearean actor and the elusive nature of his art in a wide range of different terms. The redoubtable Edmund Malone, having no direct evidence about older actors like Betterton or Barton Booth, was nonetheless "persuaded that their manner was very pompous and false, and that they spoke in a high, unnatural tone."[1] We may smile at so obvious a value judgment as this, yet modern critics sometimes appear just as unduly influenced by fixed preconceptions about the actor on Shakespeare's stage.

This controversial figure has been viewed by some in an essentially naturalistic context. "Elizabethan acting was thought at the time to be lifelike," writes one critic, thereby visualizing "a range of acting capable of greater extremes of passion, of much action which would seem forced or grotesque, but realistic within a framework of 'reality' that coincides to a large extent with ours."[2] The contrary has also been tenaciously maintained, by insisting that this style of acting was not "natural" in the sense that we understand that term today, but was basically "formalistic" and

*The author is indebted to Professor R. B. Parker of the University of Toronto for undertaking the oral presentation of this paper.
[1]J. Prior, *Life of Edmund Malone* (London, 1860), p. 345.
[2]R. A. Foakes, "The Player's Passion: Some Notes on Elizabethan Psychology and Acting," *Essays and Studies*, VII (1945), 62-77; see also Marvin Rosenberg, "Elizabethan Actors: Men or Marionettes," *PMLA*, LXIX (1954), 915-27.

"rhetorical." The difference between these two extremes, it has been argued, is that the natural actor "portrays where the formal actor symbolizes. He impersonates where the formal actor represents. He engages in real conversation where the formal actor recites. His acting is subjective and 'imaginative,' *i.e.*, he 'creates a role' where that of the formal actor is objective and traditional."[3] Still others have hailed Elizabethan acting as "epic" or as "romantic." "To this type of ceremonious acting," runs the latter view, "the heart of which was overwhelming passion intensively portrayed, neither the adjective 'formal' nor 'natural' applies. . . . Shakespeare gave his actors too rich a variety of emotions of too fine a subtlety to permit them to rely upon a stock tradition of outworn conventions."[4]

One attitude towards the whole question of Elizabethan performance is shared by virtually all modern scholars concerned with the subject; namely that the Elizabethan era was an epoch of superior acting. Yet the basis for this contention is still neither wholly agreed upon nor wholly clear, owing partly to the fact that direct evidence about the topic is too scattered and incomplete. Partly, too, lack of agreement stems from the fact that surprisingly many observers are led either to view Elizabethan acting in terms of preconceptions derived from the acting style of their own age, or else to see it as a totally isolated, unique phenomenon in the history of the theatre. A vague but compulsive need seems to be felt by many to defend, at all costs, "individuality" in the English Renaissance against the imagined threat of "conventionality." One aim of the present paper is to redirect attention to a set of predispositions and ideas about the art of acting which were prevalent in Shakespeare's England, in order thereby to restore the Elizabethan actor to his proper stylistic perspective. Nor is this pattern of aims and conventions exclusively Elizabethan; it constitutes a distinct "system" or method of approach to the art of theatrical performance which continues to shape the history of acting during the seventeenth, eighteenth, and far into the nineteenth century.

In assessing the aesthetics of Elizabethan acting, Hamlet's advice to the players assumes a central position – or, rather, continues to

[3]Alfred Harbage, *Theatre for Shakespeare* (Toronto, 1955), pp. 95-96.
[4]Bernard Beckerman, *Shakespeare at the Globe* (New York, 1962), pp. 155, 156.

occupy the celebrated position it has invariably held throughout three centuries. Since the Restoration, Hamlet's instructions have been pressed into service as arguments in support of every prevailing style of acting, always in order to justify the "naturalness" of the particular style in question. Exactly what a given age or a given person means by "natural" as an artistic quality is, of course, a point requiring careful definition if one is not to be trapped by terms. We find "naturalness" used as a criterion for the art of virtually every great actor from classical antiquity to the present day. It means little more than the manner which a particular age had come to regard as artistically correct. By themselves, then, Hamlet's directions cannot be taken as reliable evidence concerning performance style in Shakespeare's age, or any age. Hamlet's advice, as Alfred Harbage has realized, is basically a plea for quality, advocating moderation and good taste and, as such, easily suggesting to any reader the style of acting which he personally has come to consider best.[5]

Nonetheless, a closer examination of the Player speech, seen in relation to the other evidence we possess concerning the art of acting on Shakespeare's stage, reveals that this speech does, in fact, refer to certain accepted ideas and conventions. Both the specific terminology and the general frame of reference in Hamlet's instructions derive ultimately from classical sources. Thus when the Prince makes his familiar statement describing "the purpose of playing, whose end, both *at the first* and now, *was* and is, to hold, as 'twere, the mirror up to nature," he not only alludes directly to earlier acting traditions but even echoes a popular cliché of classical criticism, attributed to Cicero by Donatus in his *De Comoedia et Tragoedia* and defining comedy as "a copy of life, a mirror of custom, a reflection of truth." Other classical views concerning the art of acting permeate the remainder of the speech as well.[6]

It would be an obvious blunder to interpret the "nature" to which Hamlet refers in any modern sense. The classical and Renaissance conception of "truth to life" or verisimilitude differs radically from ours, presupposing as it does the existence of an ideal, universal truth. The classical belief that Nature consists of absolute forms which the artist is capable of imitating, as he proceeds in presenting

[5] Harbage, p. 98.
[6] Cf. the discussion in E. K. Chambers, *The Elizabethan Stage* (Oxford, 1925), I, 237-39.

active counterparts of truth through his particular medium, provides the broad foundation for an entire tradition of acting that was ultimately swept away by naturalism. "For every emotion of the mind has from nature its own peculiar look, tone, and gesture; and the whole frame of a man, and his whole countenance, and the variation of his voice function like strings in a musical instrument, just as they are moved by the affections of the mind," declared Cicero in a key passage from *De Oratore* referring both to acting and to oratory.[7] Repetitions of this same fundamental classical tenet – that there is a demonstrable link between emotion and its expression in a proper outward form, that "every passion has its peculiar and appropriate look" – are to be found in the host of treatises and practical commentaries on the subject of acting which appeared in England and on the Continent from Elizabethan and Restoration times until far into the nineteenth century.

Underlying the continuous tradition represented by these documents is the basic Ciceronian belief that the power of the actor rests in his ability to appeal to and "move the passions" of his audience by conveying human emotions in a convincing manner. To accomplish this the performer must possess both a heightened personal sensitivity and an intimate knowledge of the vocabulary of the passions. Moreover, he must be able to focus and amplify emotional expression, concentrating attention upon the vocal and physical presentation of that which is essential. The actor must select, heighten, and then individualize – this formula is fundamental to every treatise on acting style in the prenaturalistic theatre. Balancing it is the belief that the expression of heightened emotionality in declamation, gesture, and movement must be tempered by the ideals of harmonious form prevalent in each period. G. H. Lewes represents the continuity of this approach when he writes in *On Actors and the Art of Acting* (1875):

> The actor has to select. He must be typical. His expressions must be those which, while they belong to the recognized symbols of our common nature, have also the peculiar individual impress of the character represented. . . . The nearer the approach to everyday reality implied by the author in his characters and language . . . the closer must be the actor's imitation of everyday manner; but even

[7]*Cicero on Oratory and Orators*, trans. J. S. Watson (London, 1876); quoted in *Actors on Acting*, ed. Toby Cole and Helen Chinoy (New York, 1954), p. 24.

then he must idealize, *i.e.*, select and heighten – and it is for his tact to determine how much.[8]

A contrast between the system of, or approach to, acting suggested by this view and the style of performance produced by the emergence of naturalism in the 1880s and after affords perhaps a clearer illustration. Naturalistic acting – admittedly only one of many conventions in the modern theatre – is anchored in the subjective experience of the performer. The revolutionary contribution of Stanislavsky, for instance, was the development of a method whereby the actor could create an illusion of reality in a specific situation by recalling an analogous and evocative moment in his own experience. The work of the naturalistic actor with his role, concerned with experiential specificity rather than imitative ideality and carried out during rehearsals in close co-operation with a director, might be said to progress from the inside outward. In very broad terms a character is "built" of a patchwork of individual habits, idiosyncracies, and reactions to a succession of situations until the "exterior" of the character is finally established. In sharp contrast to this the older system, which the naturalistic bias discredited and displaced, led the performer to approach his role in an opposite fashion, conceiving the "outside," overall impression first and then fitting the individual responses to this conception. Appearing in plays which, of course, never pretended to mirror the surface realities of everyday life, the actor in Shakespeare's time would be concerned with the representation of idealized emotions or character impressions drawn, in the first instance, from outside himself but individualized and vitalized (in proportion to his relative ability) through the medium of his own personality. Since "truth to life" did not mean naturalism but fidelity to ideal or universal truth, the application of this principle discarded accidentals in emphasizing that which is essential in nature, and thereby focused attention on the typical in an actor's portrayal of character as well as emotion.

The Elizabethan actor, belonging to a dramatic tradition that recognized and adhered to the ideal of decorum, was trained in the depiction of characters delineated by appropriate, identifying characteristics and behaviour. We have only to recall the prologue to Richard Edwards' *Damon and Pithias*:

[8]*Actors on Acting*, p. 316.

And yet, worshipful audience, thus much I dare avouch:
In comedies the greatest skill is this: rightly to touch
All things to the quick, and eke to frame each person so
That by his common talk you may his nature rightly know.
A roister ought not preach – that were too strange to hear,
. . . .
The old man is sober; the young man rash; the lover
    triumphing in joys;
The matron grave; the harlot wild, and full of wanton toys.
. . . .
So correspondent to their kind their speeches ought to be.
Which, speeches, well-pronounc'd, with action lively framed.[9]

Clearly, however, the recognition that characters' traits must be "correspondent to their kind" was in the sense an invitation to create stereotypes. Both dramatists and performers had ample room for infinite stylistic variations within the general pattern; for those who *believed* in the principle of decorum, it was possible to vary and modulate all the more artfully within the ideal. What this principle did for the Shakespearean performer was in fact to furnish him with a readily understandable descriptive vocabulary and a flexible frame within which talented actors like Richard Burbage, Edward Alleyn, William Kemp or Richard Tarleton could move with life, freedom and individuality.

Adhering to the concept of the imitation of absolutes, the actor would be in a position to apprehend and classify not only external character traits and behaviour, but also the expression of emotions. It was the single, sustained "affection," or overall emotional impression, rather than a weave of varying individual idiosyncracies which he sought primarily to convey. Hamlet's words to the players arriving at the royal court of Elsinore suggest this: "Come, give us a taste of your quality. Come, a *passionate* speech" (II, ii). In the Elizabethan theatre (as in the classical theatre) it was accepted as a truism that a tangible and demonstrable link existed between inner emotion and its expression in outward form, or, as Thomas Wright phrased it, "that external actions as voice, and gestures, were signes of internall passions."[10] It is, therefore, not surprising to encounter such "external actions" catalogued in elaborately codified sets of rules and manuals for the expression of

[9]Joseph Quincy Adams, *Chief Pre-Shakespearean Dramas* (Cambridge, Mass., 1924), p. 572.
[10]Thomas Wright, *The Passions of the Mind* (London, 1604), p. 172; quoted in B. L. Joseph, *Elizabethan Acting* (Oxford, 1951), p. 70.

various passions. Such rules, deriving ultimately from principles set down in Cicero's *De Oratore* and Quintilian's *Institutio Oratoria*, began to appear with regularity in England from the Renaissance on. They took into account the declamation, gesture and general physical deportment of the performer as they related to the proper expression of the various dramatic affections. A characteristic instance is to be found in the preface to the anonymous play *The Cyprian Conqueror* (*c.* 1633):

> ... in a sorrowful part the head must hang down, in a proud the head must be lofty; in an amorous, closed eyes, hanging down looks and crossed arms, in a hasty, fuming and scratching the head. . . .[11]

In a wittier tone Rosalind wryly berates Orlando in *As You Like It* for his *lack* of resemblance to the ideal lover with "hanging down looks":

> A lean cheek, which you have not; a blue eye and sunken, which you have not; an unquestionable spirit, which you have not; a beard neglected, which you have not. . . . Then, your hose should be ungartered, your bonnet unbanded, your sleeve unbuttoned, your shoe untied, and everything about you demonstrating a careless desolation. (III, ii)

Shakespeare was, of course, particularly fond of using an incongruity between predictable externality and actual behaviour for his own dramatic ends. Falstaff, "written down old with all the characters of age," flaunts nature and the sensibilities of the Lord Chief Justice with his incorrigible lack of gravity:

> Have you not a moist eye, a dry hand, a yellow cheek, a white beard, a decreasing leg, an increasing belly? Is not your voice broken, your wind short, your chin double, your wit single, and every part about you blasted with antiquity, and will you yet call yourself young? Fie, fie, fie, Sir John! (2 *Henry IV*, I, ii)

A striking preoccupation with the externality of an actor's creation – his general attitude, gestures, mime and movement – recurs incessantly in the evidence concerning the art of acting in the prenaturalistic theatre, including the theatre of the Elizabethan period. Thus the criteria for Richard Burbage's greatness as an actor which emerge from the elegy on his death in 1619 unmistakably indicate that his emotional expressiveness was governed by the classical concern with a clearly delineated and harmoniously controlled external form:

[11]*Actors on Acting*, p. 90.

> ... what Roscius
> Was more to Rome than Burbage was to us:
> How to ye person he did suit his face,
> How did his speech become him, and his face
> Suit with his speech, whilst not a word did fall
> Without just weight to balance it withall.[12]

The aesthetics of Elizabethan acting carry no implication whatsoever of mechanical or puppet-like performance presented according to some rigid pattern of inviolable behaviouristic rules. Choice and use of gesture, pantomime and inflection belonged ultimately to the independent (and undirected) performer, demanding an intense personal creative involvement. The skill and conscious artistry with which the seasoned actor interpreted and individualized the objective absolutes of ideal nature determined his success.

> Oft have I seen him leape into the grave
> Suiting ye person (which he seemed to have)
> Of a sad lover, with so true an eye
> That then I would have sworn he meant to die,

continues the Burbage elegy, hinting at the manner in which the great actor individualized the spirit of "a sad lover" by means of physical appearance and behaviour.

Extant Elizabethan sets of codified rules for the suitable expression of each of the human passions may best be regarded as rules of propriety, outlining and describing basic guidelines for a convincing portrayal of emotion. These guidelines, when they refer directly to the theatre, reflect the type of highly expressive gesticulative and pantomimic vocabulary undoubtedly employed by the dramatic artists of the period. The very fact that details of these theoretical and pedagogic rules of decorum may occasionally differ somewhat regarding a specific emotion is further proof of their function. Their significance lies principally in their definition of an approach to theatrical performance, an aesthetic attitude which hinged on the belief in the vivid imitation of absolutes through the medium of formalized emotions, reactions and expressions. As the variations within the manuals indicate, the artistic frame of reference allowed for individual interpretations on the part of rhetoricians and writers as well as actors, provided that the aesthetic bounds of harmony and balance were not violated.

[12]*Ibid.,* p. 91.

Specific descriptions of how precisely to express a given affection, in terms of language, pantomime, gesture and scenic attitude, can be useful aids in visualizing the richly stylized language of plastic expression seen on the Shakespearean stage. In their search for clarity, scholars have also conjured up a wealth of stage directtions, either actual or implied, satirical references, and remarks touching upon acting in the dialogue of plays such as *Hamlet* or Marston's *Antonio's Revenge* to guide them. Unfortunately, however, the kind of additional comparative evidence, in the form of iconographic or objective critical descriptions, which could tell us how a given actor or company did in fact present particular scenes or moments in a play, is lacking. Primary evidence of this sort first becomes available in the English theatre after the Restoration, and its absence in the Elizabethan period places clear restrictions upon the kind of factual conclusions one may draw – restrictions which, of course, have never impeded the more impressionistically inclined critic from envisioning (his eyes "in a fine frenzy rolling," as Theseus would say) the precise manner in which a given company or a given actor performed (presumably on any given day one cares to choose!). For our purposes, however, the scanty evidence available must be considered quite unreliable in any *specific* instance, and is useful only because it does reveal a shared aesthetic bias shaping a general Elizabethan attitude toward the art of acting.

The modern outlook tends to find the contention that nature can be imitated, or even defined, in terms of absolute forms distasteful. As Georges May observed, in a very different context, in a recent issue of *Ventures*, "the practice of translating ideas into plastic forms according to a determined code strikes many of us today as based on an absurdly exaggerated notion of the intellectual solidarity of artists and writers."[13] Thus many critics are prone to dismiss a theory of acting dependent upon the imitation of absolutes with such effectively repellent adjectives as "hollow" and "self-conscious." Yet by choosing to ignore the sets of rules and manuals which we do possess from the Elizabethan era, these observers place themselves at a disadvantage. In discarding evidence of this sort as "academic and pedantic" or by arguing that "there was no complete agreement about the significance of a particular gesture," they allow themselves to lose sight of the wider stylistic tendency

[13]*Ventures: Magazine of the Yale Graduate School*, IX, (Fall, 1969), 64.

which these rules unquestionably illustrate – the pattern of approach that presupposed the possibility of ideal Sorrow or Fear, the existence of an ideal Lover or Tyrant.

II

In seeking to understand and interpret the fabric of aims and techniques underlying the Elizabethan approach to acting which we have been discussing, contemporary manuals of rhetoric are thus well worth re-examining in connection with other pertinent sources, particularly such works as Thomas Heywood's *An Apology for Actors* (1612) and Richard Flecknoe's *A Short Discourse of the English Stage* (1664).[14] These manuals of rhetoric include such titles as Thomas Wright's *The Passions of the Mind* (1604), Abraham Fraunce's *The Arcadian Rhetorike* (1588), and John Bulwer's *Chirologia: or, the natural language of the hand* and *Chironomia: or, the art of manuall rhetorique*, all of which have received the attention of Elizabethan scholars. Bulwer's accounts, which appeared together in 1644 and which represent the fullest treatment of rhetorical delivery in England during the Renaissance, are reliable for the Elizabethan period only to the extent that they deal directly with theatre and correspond to earlier sources. In 1649 Bulwer followed them with a work which has not enjoyed the same critical scrutiny, entitled *Pathemyotomia: or, a Dissection of the significative Muscles of the Affections of the Minde*, a truly amazing attempt to pinpoint the muscles employed in the depiction of each passion.[15]

[14]Although Flecknoe is a somewhat late document and is perhaps not based on the author's own personal observations of Elizabethan actors, it points to the same stylistic tendency as actual contemporary sources and is therefore worthy of consideration.

[15]On the flyleaf of the copy in the possession of the Yale Medical School Library an old note reads: "By far the scarcest and most curious of Bulwer's works." Bulwer would in turn be gratified by the curious scientific approval his endeavours would have enjoyed today in the new field of ethology. Recognizing that man "is able to signal his moods and thoughts with a nonverbal vocabulary of gestures and expressions," British ethologists reported in a recent issue of *New Scientist* that they had "isolated and catalogued no fewer than 135 different gestures and expressions of face, head, and body." Examples: "For appropriate warmth, the upper smile is usually enhanced by slight changes around the outer corners of the eyes. Even the broad smile is not always an entirely convincing expression of surprise or pleasure unless it is accompanied by an elevation of the eyebrows. . . . In a sad frown, the eyebrows will ordinarily be drawn down at the outer ends. By contrast, they will be depressed on the inside in an angry frown" (*Time,* June 13, 1969, 48).

It has been argued that such contemporary manuals of rhetoric continually stress the close similarity that existed between the art of the orator and that of the actor. The more precise nature of this similarity should, however, be clarified. Bulwer provides an important clue in *Chironomia*, where he explains that the art of "manuall rhetorique was first formed by Rhetoricians; afterwards amplified by Poets . . . but most strangely inlarged by Actors, the ingenious counterfeiters of mens manners. The first Romane Oratour that collected these Rhetoricall motions of the *Hand* into an Art, translating so much from the Theater to the Forum, as stood with the gravity of an Oratour, was surely Quintilian."[16] The significance of this and comparable statements by both Bulwer and Wright,[17] echoing as they do Cicero and Quintilian almost word for word, is chiefly that orators have continually profited from the example of the stage. Classical works on rhetoric instructed speakers to attempt to learn from actors by studying their gestures and mime, their intonations, and in particular their ability to convey emotion to an audience. The description of *An Excellent Actor*, which Sir Edmund Chambers attributes to John Webster, states explicitly: "Whatsoeuer is commendable in the graue Orator, is most exquisitely perfect in [the actor]; for by a full and significant action of body, he charmes our attention."[18] Flecknoe tells us that Richard Burbage "had all the parts of an excellent Orator, animating his words with speaking, and Speech with Action."[19] Thus, far from categorically "cautioning against adopting the practice of the stage," as some critics have maintained,[20] the arguments of writers like Bulwer suggest that the difference between theatrical and oratorical effect was merely one of degree. Obviously the emotional pyrotechnics of the public speaker had to be more subdued than those of the actor. However, Quintilian's admonition that "all attempts of exciting the feelings must prove ineffectual unless they

[16]J. B[ulwer], *Chironomia: or, the art of manuall rhetorique* (London, 1644), pp. 24-25.
[17]See, *e.g.*, Wright, p. 179; Sir Richard Baker, *Theatrum Triumphans* (London, 1670 [written before 1645]), p. 35; Bulwer, pp. 10-11, 17-18. If further proof is needed, the frontispiece to *Chironomia* shows two orators, Demosthenes and Cicero, being instructed in the art of gesture and pantomime by two actors, Livius Andronicus and Roscius.
[18]Quoted in A. M. Nagler, *Sources of Theatrical History* (New York, 1952), p. 126.
[19]*Ibid.*, p. 128; Chambers, IV, 370.
[20]See Alan S. Downer, "Prolegomenon to a Study of Elizabethan Acting," *Maske und Kothurn*, X (1964), 630.

be enlivened by the voice of the speaker, by his look, and by the action of his whole body" was regarded as basic to the practice of both arts.

In general, principles of rhetoric constituted one of the cornerstones of Renaissance educational philosophy; the negative and narrowing connotations which the term has somehow acquired today are totally absent from its Elizabethan meaning. Renaissance works on rhetoric were not restricted to colourful and effective speech patterns alone, but were fully as concerned with the Ciceronian "eloquence of the body" – with the contribution of movement, gesture, and pantomime to a complete and harmonious external appearance. In *The Passions of the Mind* Thomas Wright defines rhetoric as "either a certaine visible eloquence, or an eloquence of the bodie, or a comely grace in diliuering conceits, or an externall image of an internall mind, or a shadow of affections. . . . Action then vniuersally is a naturall or artificiall moderation, qualification, modification, or composition of the voice, countenance, and gesture of the bodie proceeding from some passion, and apt to stir vp the like."[21] Very likely it is to this kind of "action" of animated plastic expressiveness that the epigram "To Edward Alleyn" refers in its praise of the celebrated actor's art: "As others speak, but only thou doest act."[22]

Training in rhetorical expression was regarded in Shakespeare's age as indispensable in the education of anyone aspiring to become a fully articulated human being, capable of communicating the qualities of thought and emotion. Underlying this view and shaping the aesthetics of the prenaturalistic actor's art was the firm belief that an ideal and inescapable link existed between content or thought and its proper expression in a harmonious outward form. In Hamlet's Hecuba speech the Prince, despairing at the recognition that the natural link between inner feeling and its external display has apparently dissolved at the court in Elsinore, marvels at the connection between a feigned emotion and its proper outward expression created by the travelling player, who

> But in a fiction, in a dream of passion,
> Could force his soul so to his own conceit
> That, from her working, all his visage wann'd,
> Tears in his eyes, distraction in 's aspect,

[21]Wright, p. 176.
[22]*Actors on Acting*, p. 83.

A broken voice, and his whole function suiting
With forms to his conceit . . . (II, ii)

"And all for nothing!" continues Hamlet. "For Hecuba!" Nor was the question posed here by Shakespeare,

What's Hecuba to him, or he to Hecuba
That he should weep for her?

puzzling to this speaker alone. In a somewhat different context, Pandulpho in Marston's *Antonio's Revenge* is made to ask in his despair:

Would'st have me cry, run raving up and down
For my son's loss? Would'st have me turn rank mad,
Or wring my face with mimic action,
Stamp, curse, weep, rage, and then my bosom strike?
Away, 'tis apish action, player-like. (I, ii)

The whole notion of someone being moved by fictitious emotions is discussed at length by both Cicero and Quintilian. For these writers, as for their Elizabethan disciples, the greatest power over the emotions of others was possessed by the man susceptible and adaptable to emotional impression and the force of the imagination revealed in the work of the poet. "For *Cicero* expressly teacheth," Thomas Wright reminded his readers, "that it is almost impossible for an orator to stirre vp a passion in his auditors, except he be first affected with the same passion himselfe."[23] Prescribed guidelines for stage expression, movement, gesture, pantomime and speech in no sense implied a deliberately dispassionate or unimaginative portrayal and presumed the operation of the actor's own fantasy. His subjective identification with every phase of his role was an integral part of this philosophy of theatrical performance – for, as Cicero observed, "no fuel is so combustible as to kindle without the application of fire." "Every accent, exclamation, admiration, increpation, indignation, commiseration, abhomination, exanimation, exultation," echoed Wright, "is either a flash of fire to incense a passion, or a bason of water to quench a passion incensed."[24] This essential quality of "fire" or powerful animation brought the performance to life, carrying the passion, through the medium of the actor's own emotions, into the hearts of the spectators.

[23]Wright, p. 172.
[24]*Ibid.*, p. 175.

This principle of strength excluded, however, all indecorous elements, and strong emotion was not to be documented by what Hamlet calls "inexplicable dumb-shows and noise." As the Prince's further admonition to the players not to "out-herod Herod" indicates, the days of this medieval stage-tyrant's raging "in the pagond and in the strete also" were not too far behind. Instead, graceful scenic attitudes were the underpinning of the Elizabethan actor's art. "Be his invention never so fluent and exquisite," writes Thomas Heywood in *An Apology for Actors*, "his disposition and order never so composed and formall, his eloquence and elaborate phrases never so materiall and pithy, his memory never so firme and retentive, his pronuntiation never so musicall and plausive, yet without a comely and elegant gesture, a gratious and bewitching kinde of action, a naturall and familiar motion of the head, the hand, the body, and a moderate and fit countenance suitable to all the rest, I hold all the rest as nothing."[25] Rules of decorum aided the actor in fitting, in Heywood's words, "his phrases to his action, and his action to his phrase, and his pronuntiation to them both." Hamlet's direction advising the players to "suit the Action to the Word, the Word to the Action" (III, ii) echoes the same Ciceronian precept.

The prescribed qualities of decorum, grace, and eloquence considered essential in Elizabethan acting, and the importance of idealizing a role in conformity with prevalent concepts of the beautiful form emerge vividly in John Webster's sketch *An Excellent Actor*: "He doth not striue to make nature monstrous, she is ofen seene in the same Scaene with him, but neither on Stilts nor Crutches. . . . Hee addes grace to the Poets labours: for what in the Poet is that but ditty, in him is both ditty and music."[26] The goal of this style was not to reduplicate behaviouristic "naturalness" in the sense in which that term is understood today, but to create a structural through-line cleansed of all distracting accidentals, disfiguring blemishes, indecorous declamation, or unsuitable gestures. This goal is continually defined in the manuals of rhetoric. Thomas Wright advises orators that in observing "other men appasionat" they should "leaue the excess and exorbitant leuitie and other defects, and keepe the manner corrected with a prudent mediocritie: and this the best may be marked in stageplaiers, who act

[25]Thomas Heywood, *An Apology for Actors* (London, 1841), p. 29.
[26]Nagler, p. 126.

excellently."[27] The passions were to be restrained and contained within the ideal bounds of the Beautiful. As Hamlet exhorts the player, "in the very torrent, tempest, and . . . whirlwind of passion, you must acquire and beget a temperance, that may give it smoothness." It is not for an actor to "tear a passion to tatters, to very rags" – nor, on the other hand, should he be "too tame neither." Each action, presented clearly and forcefully to the audience, must be decorous yet animated with powerful dramatic feeling in order to appeal to the spectators' emotions.

One might contrast this ideal with another of the many images of acting woven into Shakespeare's plays. In *Troilus and Cressida* Achilles is depicted as a bad actor, a "strutting player" who brings neither grace nor decorum to his role, but who "doth think it rich/ To hear the wooden dialogue and sound/ 'Twixt his stretch'd footing and the scaffoldage" (I, iii). Actor and orator alike were expected to acquire an artistic technique which, in Heywood's terms, would enable him to "keepe a decorum in his countenance, neither to frowne when he should smile, nor to make unseemly and disguised faces in the delivery of his words . . . nor stand in his place like a livelesse image, demurely plodding, and without any smooth and formal motion." When Richard Flecknoe, in his description of "The Acting of Richard Burbage," praises Burbage as an excellent actor "never falling in his part when he had done speaking; but with his *looks* and *gesture*, maintaining it still unto the heighth,"[28] he is undoubtedly referring to that carefully regulated *jeu muet*, or "bewitching kinde of action," which from the time of the Renaissance has constituted a key aspect of the prenaturalistic theatre. We are reminded of the production of *Othello* by the King's Men in 1610 in which the performers "moved the audience to tears, not only by their speech, but by their gestures as well." The portrayal of Desdemona was especially effective, we are told, "when she lay in bed, moving the spectators to pity solely by her face."[29] Similarly Fynes Moryson's comments about the ragged troupe of English comedians who performed in Frankfort in 1592 and thoroughly impressed audiences with their mimic ability come to mind: "Both men and women flocked wonderfully to see theire gesture and Action, rather than heare them, speaking English

[27]Wright, p. 179.
[28]Nagler, p. 128; Chambers, IV, 370. My italics.
[29]Quoted in A. M. Nagler, *Shakespeare's Stage* (New Haven, 1958), p. 82.

which they understood not."[30] In general, the comparative wealth of evidence dealing with graceful physical attitudes, movements, and gestures suggests a pervading concern with the visual aspects of performance on the Shakespearean stage. The familiar Elizabethan penchant for dumb-shows and processions coincided with a concentrated effort by rhetoricians to formulate systems of facial expressions, and body movements corresponding to each of the passions.

Bulwer expounds at length on the necessity for correctly employed illustrative gestures with which to convey the passions. We are continually reminded by him that correct use of gesticulation is indispensable to a decorous and credible dramatic effect. "To use no Action at all in speaking," he warns, "or a heavy or slow motion of the *Hand*, is the propertie of one stupid and sluggish."[31] Bulwer goes on to provide plates in his works which copiously and concretely illustrate his view of *how* the arms, hands, and fingers should be incorporated in rhetorical delivery. Occasionally he makes specific reference to the more intensified nature of the actor's art: "The Breast stricken with the *Hand*, is an action of *Griefe, sorrow, repentance*, and indignation. . . . A vehement percussion of the breast is not convenient [for public speakers], but is to be remitted to the Theater." In comparing these more vehement theatrical "actions" to those of the orator, Bulwer further informs us that "the Forehead stricken with the *Hand*, is an action of *dolour, shame*, and *admiration* . . . worthy of banishment from the Hand of an Oratour, and to be confined to the Theater." Similarly, "the trembling *Hand* is scenicall, and belongs more to the theater, then [*sic*] the forum."[32] No one would seriously suggest that Bulwer's rules for passions were necessarily copied literally on the stage, but the general artistic bias which they represent, corresponding as it does to a continuous tradition also echoed in Hamlet's advice to the players, is basic and important.

The close correspondence which was felt to exist between human passions and their idealized expression in external form did not preclude the fact that the nature of this expression varied to reflect the kind of character portrayed. As described earlier, a

[30]See J. Isaacs, "Shakespeare as Man of the Theatre," *Shakespeare Criticism 1919-1935*, ed. Anne Ridler (Oxford, 1936), p. 296.
[31]Bulwer, *Chironomia*, p. 115.
[32]See *ibid.*, pp. 46-50.

basic principle of this approach to acting was to conceive the over-all impression of a role first and then to fit the appropriate individual responses to this conception. Meaning was to be conveyed in terms of a clearly defined, total characterization. Hence the selection and intensive use of prescribed gesticulation expressed not merely a range of human emotions but also served to identify specific dramatis personae. In this sense, Heywood's *Apology for Actors* emphasizes the necessity of qualifying "every thing according to the nature of the person presented."[33] Just as noble bearing, in compliance with Renaissance ideals of the beautiful form, was indicated by graceful facility of gesture, so its opposite was denoted by the comparative absence of these accomplishments:

> They who have *Hands* slow and ponderous, and who without any comelinesse beare and offer about their leaden *Hands*, together with the arms, after a rusticall manner; so lifting it up sometimes, that they seeme to move a great lumpe of trembling flesh, reaching their slow Right hand out so timorously, as if they gave provender to an Elephant. Such are by this customary habit, discovered to be Clownes.[34]

In Bulwer's characterization of the clown does one not detect a hint of that "sanguine coward," that "huge hill of flesh," Sir John Falstaff?

No matter which passion or which type of character was to be depicted, however, the principal objective remained, in Hamlet's words, "this special observance, that you o'erstep not the modesty of nature" – that is, that the actor should not violate the Elizabethan conception of a properly controlled and harmonious appearance. This is the context for Hamlet's specific instruction to the players regarding gesticulation: "Nor do not saw the air too much with your hand, thus, but use all gently." In how literal a sense this practical hint is meant emerges from the fact that Hamlet's piece of advice, which is re-stated as a principle in

[33]Heywood, p. 30. An even clearer statement of this principle is provided by Charles Gildon in his *Life of Mr. Thomas Betterton, the Late Eminent Tragedian* (1710): "A patriot, a prince, a beggar, a clown, etc., must each have their propriety, and distinction in action as well as words and language. An actor therefore must vary with his argument, that is, carry the person in all his manners and qualities with him in every action and passion" (*Actors on Acting*, pp. 99-100).
[34]Bulwer, *Chironomia*, p. 117.

Bulwer[35] and in a wide range of other acting manuals during the next two centuries, actually paraphrases Quintilian's disapproving warning: "*Solet esse et pigra et trepida et secanti similis* – there are others, again, whose hands are sluggish or tremulous or inclined to saw the air."[36] The aesthetic justification for this venerable rule of theatrical craftsmanship is touched upon in *Chironomia*: "Shun similitude of gesture; for as a monotonie in the voice; so a continued similitude of gesture, and a *Hand* always playing upon one string is absurd."[37]

On the Elizabethan stage it must have been the variety and finesse with which superior actors personalized and projected each gesture and movement in close, expressive harmony with their delivery that constituted their art. "The *Hand* with a gentle percussion, now greater, now lesse; now flat, now sharpe, according to the diversities of the affections, is fitted to *distinguish the Comma's & breathing parts of a sentence*."[38] Nothing in this lively art seems intended to be inflexible, stilted, or marionette-like. "A Play *read*, hath not half the pleasure of a Play acted," Sir Richard Baker reminds us, "for though it have the pleasure of *ingenious Speeches*; yet it wants the pleasure of *Gracefull action*: and we may well acknowledg, that *Gracefulness of action*, is the greatest pleasure of a Play."[39]

III

Turning lastly to the most elusive feature of all, stage delivery, we may perhaps find it even more difficult to imagine how an actor sounded on Shakespeare's stage than to envision his actions and gestures. Here again, however, would not the aesthetic criteria of the period, the emphasis upon form, and the cultivation of conscious artifice and beauty of expression all seem to point to a predominantly stylized delivery? Such an assumption receives added support from the convention of assigning female roles to boy actors. When Hamlet requests the players to "speak the speech . . . trippingly on the tongue," he too seems to be advocat-

[35]*Ibid.*, pp. 102-03.
[36]Quintilian, *Institutio Oratoria*, Loeb Classical Library (Cambridge, Mass., 1921-22), IV, 306-07.
[37]Bulwer, *Chironomia*, p. 136.
[38]*Ibid.*, p. 44.
[39]Baker, pp. 34-35.

ing a carefully studied, regulated style, not a naturalistic approach dependent on the rhythms of common speech. The Prince singles out for particular condemnation the kind of uncontrolled players who:

> neither having the accent of Christians, nor the gait of a Christian, pagan, nor man, have so strutted and bellowed that I have thought some of Nature's journeymen had made men, and not made them well, they imitated humanity so abominably.

The manuals of rhetoric and the other sources referring specifically to acting appear to lay stress upon a heightened, artful, even musical diction. Flecknoe, writing somewhat later, describes Burbage in terms which one would normally associate with an opera singer: "there being as much difference between him and one of our common Actors, as between a Ballad-singer who only mouths it, and an excellent singer, who knows all the Graces, and can artfully vary and modulate his Voice, even to know how much breath to give to every syllable."[40] His description corresponds remarkably well with the terminology of an Elizabethan rhetorician like Abraham Fraunce who, for certain kinds of passages, expressly advocates "that pleasant and delicate tuning of the voice, which resembleth the consent and harmonie of some well orderd song."[41]

Surely we must reject, on the other hand, the notion that the Elizabethan performer used his voice merely to declaim in a musically pleasing fashion, coolly pointing up salient figures of speech and conceits with no attempt at incorporating his declamation into the interpretation of his role, as a tangible manifestation of the person speaking. Much of the evidence in the foregoing has already demonstrated that declamation could not have been isolated from character depiction but was regarded as an integral part of the actor's total dramatic portrayal. As in the case of gesture and pantomime, specific modes of speech were directly associated with the proper expression of particular passions and reactions in a part. Thus, relying on Julius Pollux as a suitable classical authority, the unknown author of *The Cyprian Conqueror* provides in his preface a list of speech modes that include: "a narrow voice, which is so that the auditors' ears are filled with it . . . a confused voice, so that the articulate sound is not distinct . . . a rude, rough, or

---

[40]Nagler, p. 128; Chambers, IV, 370.
[41]Abraham Fraunce, *The Arcadian Rhetorike*, ed. Ethel Seaton (Oxford, 1950), p. 107.

blunt voice . . . a careless voice . . . a foolish unapt to persuade . . . harsh and sharp . . . sad, amorous, and bitter . . . infirm and weak . . . loud shrill."[42] Fraunce argues that in displaying affections the voice must be managed "diversely, according to the varietie of passions that are to be expressed," proceeding thereafter to offer specific guidelines, such as: "in pitie and lamentation, the voyce must be full, sobbing, flexible, interrupted."[43] Such catalogues of specific vocal inflections and tones, drawn up to correspond to a range of human temperaments and emotions, are significant as products of the Renaissance conceptions of decorum and due proportion, and of the belief in a demonstrable link between inner thought or emotion and its ideal outward manifestations. They should not be viewed as collections of stereotyped mannerisms to be slavishly imitated in monotonous fashion; as Cicero originally phrased it, they were put forward in rhetorical writings in the same spirit "as colors to the painter, to produce variety." The lively improvisations of the clown obviously required quite different qualities of speech and action than the more ceremonial and sober demeanour of his nobler superiors in the performance.

The stylistic subtlety which is a hallmark of Elizabethan drama and the very nature of the plays themselves seem almost perforce to demand from the actor both an intelligent reading of his part and a virtuoso-like delivery – one in no way resembling that illustrious prologue speech by Quince in *A Midsummer Night's Dream* which appeared "like a tangled chain, nothing impaired, but all disordered" (V, i). Were one forced to choose, Heywood for one preferred cerebral to vocal ability in candidates for the profession: "they should be rather schollars, that, though they cannot speake well, know how to speake, or else to have that volubility that they can speake well, though they understand not what . . . but where a good tongue and a good conceit both faile, there can never be a good actor."[44] In any case, the matchless and challenging variety of Elizabethan dramaturgy – its rich blend of dramatic modes and varied shadings of tone, speech pattern, and characterization – made a correspondingly wide range of variations desirable in the stage realization of the plays. The acting ability

[42]*Actors on Acting*, pp. 89-90.
[43]Fraunce, p. 107; Beckerman, p. 115.
[44]Heywood, pp. 43-44.

of the Elizabethan virtuoso, grounded in a skilfully regulated technique and a harmoniously controlled form of presentation, enabled him to meet the challenge represented by this dramatic variety with creative imagination and vitality.

To achieve a meaningful understanding of Elizabethan acting – or, for that matter, of the acting style of any period – one must in the last analysis eschew the imposition of current values or preconceptions or aberrations produced by wishful thinking. It has been the aim of this paper, which relies not upon freshly unearthed evidence (for from whence should such come, if it is not to be "invented" as in Alfred Harbage's delightful "discovery" of Shakespeare letters?[45]) but upon a reassessment of, for the most part, familiar documents, to approach Elizabethan acting in its own terms, recalling the restatement of classical values and aims in the European Renaissance which so profoundly influenced its development. The Elizabethan performer created his roles within the perimeters of an aesthetic system founded on the fundamental classical belief that Nature consists of absolute forms which the artist, by presenting active counterparts of truth through his own medium, brings to life. Proceeding from the assumption that "every emotion of the mind has from nature its own peculiar look, tone, and gesture," the actor created in his own image convincing and undistorted counterparts of these objective emotions, reactions, and "affections of the mind." In this way his artistry shared the wider classical concern with form in the arts, with completeness of outline, and with the subjugation of the individual detail to the harmonious design of the whole.

[45]In Alfred Harbage, *Conceptions of Shakespeare* (Cambridge, Mass., 1966).

A Shakespearean Experiment:
The Dramaturgy of
Measure for Measure

BERNARD BECKERMAN

In the second scene of *Measure for Measure* Mistress Overdone informs Lucio and his companions that "within these three days" Claudio's head is to be chopped off. This line introduces the factor of time into the dramatic action. During the next two scenes no further mention is made of Claudio's impending death. But with the first scene of Act II Shakespeare begins a refrain of urgency. Angelo initiates it with his order to the Provost: "See that Claudio/ Be executed by nine tomorrow morning" (33-34). In Act II, scene ii, the refrain becomes insistent. The Provost inquires, "Is it your will Claudio shall die tomorrow?" "Did not I tell thee, yea?" retorts Angelo (7-8). Angelo tells Isabella that Claudio "must die tomorrow" (82) and again later, "Your brother dies tomorrow" (106). Next the Duke asks the Provost, "When must [Claudio] die?" The Provost answers, "As I do think, tomorrow" (II.iii.16). Later in the scene the Duke tells Juliet, "Your partner, as I hear, must die tomorrow" (37). She echoes him three lines later, "Must die tomorrow!" During the second encounter between Isabella and Angelo the time of Claudio's death is not mentioned. Angelo instead warns Isabella, "Answer me tomorrow" whether or not she will trade her chastity for Claudio's life. The refrain, taken up by Isabella, recommences in the prison scene. She tells Claudio, "Tomorrow you set on" (III.i.60). And later: "This night's the time/ That I should do what I abhor to name,/ Or else thou diest tomorrow" (100-102). And again, a few lines later: "Be ready,

Claudio, for your death tomorrow" (106). The echo reverberates with the Duke's "tomorrow you must die" (III.i.168), and Escalus', "Claudio must die tomorrow" (III.ii.202). In Act IV, the temporal pressure becomes more specific. The Provost advises Abhorson, "Tomorrow morning are to die Claudio and/ Barnardine" (IV.ii. 3-7), and gives him Pompey to help [him] "tomorrow" in his execution (20-21). Shortly after, he orders Abhorson to "provide your block and your axe tomorrow four o'clock" (51-52). He tells Claudio,

> Look, here's the warrant, Claudio, for thy death.
> 'Tis now dead midnight, and by eight tomorrow
> Thou must be made immortal. (61-62)

The Duke echoes the old refrain when he asks, "Have you no countermand for Claudio yet,/ But he must die tomorrow?" (90-91). There follows a series of references to the coming dawn and the exact hour of execution. The last two remarks in the play about that indefinite morrow occur when the Duke advises Isabella that "The Duke comes tomorrow" (IV.iii.127), and thirty lines later when Lucio reports a rumour to the same effect. In the fifth act the action occurs in a vitalized present, for specific temporal references are to the morn after Isabella's supposed assignation with Angelo (104), to "yesternight" in the prison (137), to "five years since" (216), to "Tuesday night last gone" (228) – in short, to the past.

Shakespeare's iteration of "tomorrow" in Acts II to IV and his recollection of the past in Act V have nothing whatever to do with actual time. Taken literally, the temporal sequence of the play is chronologically impossible, and it is misplaced effort to attempt either to justify the events naturalistically or to argue corruption of the text from it, as the New Cambridge editors do.[1] They claim that the discrepancy between the various hours set for Claudio's execution proves such corruption. But this discrepancy is apparent only to those who ignore dramatic and insist on clock time. The mention of an exact hour must be heard against the refrain of "tomorrow." The only time an hour is specified without being linked to tomorrow is in the letter Angelo sends to the Provost. There the Provost finds the injunction to execute Claudio "by four

William Shakespeare, *Measure for Measure*, eds. Sir Arthur Quiller-Couch and J. D. Wilson (Cambridge: University Press, 1922), p. 159. In the recent Arden edition of the play (1965), J. W. Lever disputes those critics who base theory of textual corruption on temporal discrepancies (pp. xiv-xvii).

of the clock" and send his head to Angelo "by five" (IV.ii. 119-21)
Earlier, the Provost ordered Abhorson to provide the block by
"tomorrow four o'clock." This was a general order, not applicable
to Claudio alone, but including Barnardine. Shortly thereafter the
Provost warned Claudio that he must die by "eight tomorrow."
Thus the time between four and eight is crucial to Claudio. Angelo's messenger, on departing, observes that "it is almost day"
(104), indicating that he has delivered Angelo's letter at the
moment the execution is ordered and at a time Abhorson is supposedly ready. After the Duke convinces the Provost to let Barnardine "this morning" be executed (169), he notes "the unfolding
star calls up the shepherd" (202-203), and by the end of the scene
that it is "almost clear dawn" (209). This cluster of exact temporal
references produces an impression of slow motion as the minutes
of the night gradually pass. What seems to be a discrepancy is
actually an artful way of combining melodramatic pressure with
an illusion of uncertainty about the future, an uncertainty that
continues until it is allayed when the Duke comes "home tomorrow."

Clearly, the action of *Measure for Measure* occurs in a dramatic
time of the imminent future and the achieved present. The firm
control of this factor in the play is evident. Moreover, it encom-
passes the play as a whole, demonstrating the care with which
Shakespeare developed his material. To my mind it is contributing
evidence that Shakespeare exerted artistic discretion over his
entire work, and it is with that assumption that I explore Shakespeare's dramaturgy in *Measure for Measure*.

The central fact about *Measure for Measure* which we must ex-
plicate if we are to engage in close analysis of the play is its radical
shift in character during Act III, scene i. "The play is not of a
piece," insists Professor Tillyard, "but changes its nature half-way
through."[2] This shift is manifested in three ways. First, there is a
sudden change from poetry to prose, not occasioned by introduction of low comedy characters or frivolous subject matter but
effected by the mere will of the dramatist. Second, there is a narrative change. The first half focuses upon the Angelo-Isabella-
Claudio relationship; the second half concentrates upon the Duke
and his schemes. Third, the tone of the play moves from grave con-

[2]E. M. W. Tillyard, *Shakespeare's Problem Plays* (Toronto: University of
Toronto Press, 1950), p. 123.

frontations of a semi-tragic intensity to melodramatic manipulation of sordid intrigue. These are the facts of the action. How can we account for them?

The way we go about answering this question may be more significant than what the answer itself may be. One method is to deny or minimize the facts, to find an overriding interpretation that explains the play as a whole and, therefore, obviates the necessity to recognize the dramatic shift. The interpretation may be theological, ethical, or topical. Each of these approaches had and still has considerable influence over our understanding of *Measure for Measure*. For a time it was fashionable to see the Duke as the Incarnated Lord and Lucio as his Satanic Adversary.[3] Less doctrinaire but no less influential is the ethical concept of *Measure for Measure*. Its centre is the conflict of Justice and Mercy; its action, the allegory of unerring Justice and unerring Truth battling false Authority.[4] Linked in spirit but independent in argument is the topical interpretation that the Duke, as the ideal ruler, is the theatrical evocation of the governing policy of James I.[5] Admittedly, these three schools of interpretation have led scholars to enlarge our understanding of Elizabethan moral, legal, and matrimonial views. But the advocates of the theological, ethical, and topical interpretations share one methodological weakness. They deal with general ideas and implications stimulated by the statements of the characters rather than by the experience projected through a sequence of events. They deal with matters that serve as background to the action rather than the action itself. The criticism that Roland Frye levels at the theological arguments advanced by the school of G. Wilson Knight might well apply to the other two approaches as well. He charges that Knight's followers tend to move "further and further from the play itself and from its rootage in history, until the play eventually becomes not the controlling datum of their discussion but rather a mere point of

[3]G. Wilson Knight, "*Measure for Measure* and the Gospels," in *The Wheel of Fire* (New York: Meridian Books, rev. ed., 1957), first published, 1930; Nevill Coghill, "Comic Form in *Measure for Measure*," *Shakespeare Survey* 8 (1955).
[4]M. C. Bradbrook, "Authority, Truth and Justice in *Measure for Measure*," *Review of English Studies*, XVII (1941), 385-399; Ernest Schanzer, *The Problem Plays of Shakespeare* (London: Routledge & Kegan Paul, 1936).
[5]Josephine Waters Bennett, *Measure for Measure as Royal Entertainment* (New York: Columbia University Press, 1966); Herbert Howarth, "Shakespeare's Flattery in *Measure for Measure*," *Shakespeare Quarterly*, XVI (1965), 29-37.

departure for subjective reverie and reflection."[6]

The essential assumption in all these approaches is that an accurate image of *Measure for Measure* can be gained by unearthing parallels between Shakespeare's text and contemporary Elizabethan or pre-Elizabethan works on law, matrimony, or religion. Usually, the parallels tend to be general. Sometimes, however, a critic endeavours to show that Shakespeare paraphrases a specific source. For example, Knight claims to find echoes of the gospels in *Measure for Measure* although only one of the nine parallels he cites can indeed be soundly defended.[7] The same objection can be directed against Josephine Bennett's contention that the political views of Duke Vincentio are reflections of those set down by James I in his *Basilikon Doron*. What is at fault with the habit of parallelism, whether specific, as in these last two examples, or general, as in most instances, is first, that it is highly selective and next, that it is exclusively verbal. By being highly selective, the critic can always find some passages that will vaguely suggest echoes of a source in the play. By being exclusively verbal, the critic can ignore the essential nature of the play as an artistic creation. Not that one should neglect the relevance of Renaissance ideas to *Measure for Measure*, but rather one should properly relate such ideas to the dramatic form of the work.

There is no question that ideas on justice and mercy abound in *Measure for Measure*. To a large extent they are its subject in the same way that the Trojan war is the subject of *Troilus and Cressida*. But Shakespeare does not attempt to write a historical commentary on that war. Instead he uses history as a background to human action. Just so do the conflicting claims of justice and mercy serve as a provocative background for the fictive natures of Angelo, Isabella, and the Duke. As Elizabeth Pope demonstrates, Shakespeare confines himself to conventional notions of justice and mercy.[8] Surely, his purpose could not have been the mere recital of these commonplaces. Rather he sought to dramatize ways in which

---

[6]Roland Mushat Frye, *Shakespeare and Christian Doctrine* (Princeton, N.J.: Princeton University Press, 1963), p. 20.

[7]Knight, "*Measure for Measure* and the Gospels." Virtually all nine are of the most general sort, only one truly illustrating verbal echoes (light of Angelo's character [I.i.311-32] = light of candle [Matthew, v. 14], quoted by Knight, p. 77).

[8]Elizabeth Pope, "The Renaissance Background of *Measure for Measure*," *Shakespeare Survey 2* (1949), p. 80.

uman beings interact with each other, using everyday conceptions
f justice and mercy as raw subject matter for that interaction.
Illuminating as the Renaissance ideas may prove, they are properly
he background for the play. In the forefront is the narrative action.

It is when the action is in the forefront of our attention that we
annot ignore the radical change of style in Act III, scene i. With
ew exceptions,[9] critics who have directed their attention to that
hange regard it as evidence that Shakespeare faltered in complet-
ng the play. Walter Pater intimates that it is a sign of "flagging
kill." "The play, though still not without traces of nobler handi-
work, sinks down ... into homely comedy, and it might be supposed
hat just here the grander manner deserted it."[10] The imputation,
arely hinted at by Pater but more explicitly stated by other critics
uch as Quiller-Couch, Tillyard, Marco Mincoff, and Philip Edwards,[11] is that Shakespeare either lost interest in his creation or
ost the ability to shape it. But the authors of these views find that
hey must modify their observations since they admit, for the most
art, that the fifth act is artfully wrought and masterfully executed.
Consequently, it is necessary to posit a revival of interest on Shakespeare's part, leading to an arbitrary assumption of fragmented
composition rather than to a coherent estimate of the play.

Personally, I doubt that Shakespeare lost interest in *Measure for
Measure* or that its failure, to the degree that there is failure, can
be attributed to "flagging skill" in the ordinary sense. The dramatic
elements are too completely controlled. I have already cited the
efrain that Claudio must die "tomorrow" as evidence of Shakespeare's imaginative plan. The same conscious control can be seen
n his handling of prose and poetry. He deliberately prepares for
he dramatic shift by intermixing prose and poetry subtly in the
econd scene of the play. Until the major shift in Act III, there are
wo passages of prose, mainly that between Lucio and the gentle-

---

David Lloyd Stevenson, *The Achievement of Shakespeare's Measure for
Measure* (Ithaca, N.Y.: Cornell University Press, 1966), pp. 46ff. Stevenson
ases his argument that Act III, scene i is a unified whole on a psychological
analysis of Isabella.

[10]Walter Pater, "*Measure for Measure*," in *Appreciations* (London: Macmillan
and Co., Ltd., 1904), pp. 178-79.

[11]Sir Arthur Quiller-Couch, Introduction to New Cambridge edition of
Measure for Measure, p. xxxix; Tillyard, *passim*; Marco Mincoff, "*Measure for
Measure*: A Question of Approach," *Shakespeare Studies*, II (1966), p. 145;
Philip Edwards, *Shakespeare and the Confines of Art* (London: Methuen &
Co., Ltd., 1968), p. 119.

men (I.ii.1-40) and that between Escalus and the "comic" charac
ters (II.i.41-276). The contrast of tone between the dignity of th
opening verses of the Duke and the ribald wit of Lucio provide
the musical key to the entire play. Until the Duke addresses Isa
bella in Act III, he does not speak a word of prose. Then suddenly
his lines no longer keep their measured step but turn to a mor
casual rhythm. After this major shift, Shakespeare gradually re
introduces poetic passages, never quite abandoning passages i
prose, but allowing the poetic form to dominate. Where and wh
he introduces verse passages in the third and fourth acts will b
considered subsequently. At this point it is enough, I believe, t
note the skilful modulation of his style. It leads me to accept th
division of the play into two halves as a deliberate artistic choice
If it is such a deliberate choice, as I suggest, then what does tha
tell us about the play?

To answer this question, we need to glance, however cursorily
at Shakespeare's practice in other plays. The once prevailing notio
that Elizabethan dramatic form existed only as a poetic mediun
and that Shakespeare's achievements can be appreciated solely o
the poetic plane, is yielding to the recognition of the special narra
tive artistry that characterizes his best work. One feature of thi
artistry that I have discussed elsewhere,[12] and that is of principa
concern for us here, is its "split structure." I apply the term to th
manner in which a precipitating event is raised to a plateau o
sustained reactions at the play's centre and then succeeded b
narrative complications. In *Julius Caesar* the precipitating event i
Caesar's triumph and the need for Brutus to respond to it. Th
conspiracy against Caesar, of which Brutus' response is central
reaches its fullest elaboration in the assassination and funera
scenes. Thereafter, the action changes direction.

Two specific features of the split structure may be noted. First
unlike classical form the play's action, as it progresses towards th
centre, does not move to revelation, confrontation, or complication
That is why it is inappropriate to apply such a term as *epitasis* t
this centre. Instead the developing action propels the character
into situations where sustained emotional and imaginative reac
tions are produced. Thus the pattern is not the classical one of in

[12]*Shakespeare at the Globe* (New York: Macmillan, 1962), chapter II
Dynamics of Drama: Theory and Method of Analysis (New York: Knopf
1970), chapter V.

creasing constriction where characters become entrapped, but the Elizabethan one of expansion through which characters are hurtled into moral chaos. Second, again unlike the classical form, the centre of the play is not a single moment. In discussions of rising and falling action, classically-oriented theorists usually envision a shift from one to the other as an instance of time, as a turning point or a climax. The concept of such an instance owes its origin to the Aristotelian notion of *peripeteia* or reversal. In Shakespeare, however, that type of reversal rarely exists. Instead, there is, as I noted, an elaboration of a narrative sequence into a series of heightened passages mainly in the third act. These passages may be clearly seen in *Macbeth* and *King Lear*. In both plays the impelling forces provoke extreme mental and emotional states, in Macbeth driving him from fear to monstrousness and in Lear to a complete breakdown.

In Shakespeare's treatment of this narrative form, the third act or "climactic plateau" consists of an elaboration of passion. Narrative complication is reduced and room is left for heightened emotional states. Often, as in Macbeth's double response to Banquo's ghost, the same passionate reaction recurs with equal or augmented intensity. Once the reaction is completed, several dramatic and psychological shifts occur. There is a re-emphasis upon narrative development and complication. Often the leading character disappears from the action for a number of scenes. Through these practices Shakespeare creates an impression of elapsed time and altered mood. When next a leading character appears, he seems to have undergone a transformation. The fire of the climactic sequence is banked, and although passion is present, it lacks the unbridled force of its earlier state. These characteristics may be seen most clearly in *Hamlet, Macbeth*, and *King Lear*, less fully in *Julius Caesar*, but are present in general outline in all the tragedies.

Shakespeare's use of this narrative pattern in the tragedies illuminates *Measure for Measure*, I believe. But his use of it in *The Winter's Tale* is even more revealing. In the tragedies, the shift from the elaboration of passion to new plotting is primarily a narrative shift. *The Winter's Tale*, on the other hand, exhibits not only a *narrative* shift but a *tonal* one as well. The first half of the play deals with Leontes' passionate jealousy, one almost tragic in quality; the second half dramatizes a romantic and pastoral story of young love endangered and old love restored. This change in tone is produced not only by the introduction of new story material and by a lapse of time but by a technique that we have already encountered in *Measure for Measure*, namely, the alternation of prose and verse.

The first half of *The Winter's Tale* is largely in verse, the second half substantially in prose mixed with verse. For example, the first scene is in prose, the next five through Act III, scene ii wholly in verse, except for the indictment against Hermione (III.ii.12-21) and the oracle of Apollo (III.ii.132-35). Act III, scene iii is split: the first fifty-eight lines being in verse, the remaining sixty-five in prose. A shift of action occurs between the two. Antigonus abandons Perdita and exits "pursued by a bear"; the old shepherd and clown enter to find the child. Destruction ends and renewal commences. The chorus of Time, immediately following, is in verse (32 lines). The next two scenes are in prose, and the rest of the play alternates between prose and verse, the concluding scene in verse succeeding a scene fully in prose. The deliberateness of this pattern shows the same attention that Shakespeare gave to *Measure for Measure*, and together with the radical shift in tone, suggests that in *Measure for Measure* Shakespeare experimented with a dramatic arrangement that he more fully developed in *The Winter's Tale*.

Thus, we can see that the schizophrenic form of *Measure for Measure* is not peculiar to this play alone but is rooted in Shakespeare's dramaturgic method. In *Measure for Measure*, however, there are certain distinctive features. Along with *The Winter's Tale*, *Measure for Measure* shares not only the narrative shift common to many plays but also a tonal and verbal shift. The deliberateness of this shift in *Measure for Measure* and its repetition, more adroitly I believe, in *The Winter's Tale*, argues Shakespeare's desire to create a novel dramatic effect. Perhaps we can discern that effect by close scrutiny of the narrative structure.

Two precipitating events initiate the action: the Duke's departure and Claudio's arrest. The purpose prompting the departure is crucial, but equivocally presented. Coghill and Dickinson argue that the Duke leaves Vienna in the care of Angelo in order to test him and that, in fact, the play is a series of tests imposed on the characters.[13] The clearest evidence for this interpretation can be found in the Duke's lines to Friar Thomas:

[13]Nevill Coghill, "Comic Form in *Measure for Measure*," p. 19; John W. Dickinson, "Renaissance Equity and *Measure for Measure*," *Shakespeare Quarterly*, XIII (1926), 294.

> Moe reasons for this action [his departure and disguise]
> At our more leisure shall I render you;
> Only this one: Lord Angelo is precise;
> Stands at a guard with Envy; scarce confesses
> That his blood flows; or that his appetite
> Is more to bread than stone. Hence shall we see
> If powers change purpose, what our seemers be. (I. iii. 48-54)

Stevenson sees the motive of testing balanced by the Duke's sense of having been remiss as a ruler, thus producing a "teasing ambiguity" at the opening of the play.[14] But the ambiguity is more apparent than real. Coming as the speech does at the end of a scene, it bears a decided resemblance to Hal's confession that he will awhile uphold "the unyoked humour" of Falstaff's idleness, for although the Duke is preparing us for his later testing of Angelo, the test itself is a by-product of his principal intent which is to purge the commonwealth. This is confirmed when the Duke's words are measured against his behaviour and his attitudes toward Escalus, Angelo, Claudio, and Juliet.

The Duke imposes the office of ruler upon a reluctant man. He calls on Angelo to express his full nature in the way he exerts authority.

> Your scope is as mine own,
> So to enforce or qualify the laws
> As to your soul seems good. (I. i. 64-66)

That the Duke concurs with Angelo's subsequent acts as governor is made manifest by the way Shakespeare introduces the motif of rigorous law enforcement. This motif is first raised by Claudio who is baffled by the reason for Angelo's harsh judgment against him. Whether the cause lies in the very position of a ruler or in the personality of this particular ruler, he cannot tell. In the very next scene the Duke resolves this quandary. He tells Friar Thomas that he chose Lord Angelo, "a man of stricture and firm abstinence," because he wished to have law strictly imposed as a remedy for his own failures. Until now the Duke has let the "biting laws" sleep, to such an extent that his decrees

> Dead to infliction, to themselves are dead,
> And Liberty plucks Justice by the nose. (I. iii. 28-29)

Angelo's rigour will correct this delinquency. Consequently, An-

[14]Stevenson, p. 35.

gelo's "tyranny" or strictness is both in the ruler's position as well as in the "eminence that fills it up" because the Duke has wedded the one to the other. This point is reinforced by the first words we next hear Angelo speak. He echoes the very sentiments enunciated by the Duke.

> We must not make a scarecrow of the law,
> Setting it up to fear the birds of prey,
> And let it keep one shape, till custom make it
> Their perch and not their terror. (II. i. 1-4)

Through such successive parallelism Shakespeare links the Duke's wish to Angelo's action.

This view, that the Duke is motivated not by Angelo's nature but by his own errors, is not universally accepted. For those who see the Duke as an ideal ruler, his trust in Angelo is merely a subterfuge. His true reflection, according to Ernest Schanzer and Mary Lascelles, is Escalus.[15] For these writers Escalus represents the finest qualities of the balance of justice and mercy, and his interrogation of Pompey is cited as an example of exemplary judgment. The sequence of behaviour in Act II, scene i, however, does not support such a theory. The scene starts with Escalus' attempt to persuade Angelo to be moderate. He introduces a motif to be taken up later by Isabella, querying whether Angelo might himself not have succumbed to temptation (8-16). The introduction of Elbow, Froth and Pompey provides occasion for Escalus to illustrate the administration of justice. He disposes of Froth neatly enough, but his private questioning of Pompey is less effective. More to the point, in his decision on Pompey, Escalus illustrates the very thing the Duke had always done: sticking "the threatening twigs of birch" in his subjects' sight, but not using them. Though made to look a fool by Pompey, Escalus is certainly not a fool. He realizes his failure at the end of the scene when a figure called Justice echoes Escalus' plea for moderation by asserting, "Lord Angelo is severe." Now, however, Escalus adopts a different tone, repeating the motif sounded by the Duke and Angelo previously. Severity, he says, is needful,

> Mercy is not itself, that oft looks so;
> Pardon is still the nurse of second woe. (II. i. 280-81)

[15]Mary Lascelles, *Shakespeare's Measure for Measure* (London: The Athlone Press, 1953), pp. 62-63; Schanzer, p. 115. Also Dickinson, see n. 13.

Why the Duke chose Angelo over Escalus is now apparent. Escalus is too much like him. Although Escalus can see the need for rigour, he vacillates, lamenting, "yet poor Claudio." Escalus clearly embodies the lenient way, which the Duke now rejects, and Angelo the stern way, to which the Duke now turns.

The second precipitating event of the play is Claudio's arrest. Claudio is to be punished for fornication. Mitigating circumstances exist, for he is ready to marry Juliet and was indeed betrothed to her. To decide whether their contract was *de praesenti*, as Schanzer argues, or *de futuro*, as Nagarajan claims,[16] may assist us in appreciating fine points of Elizabethan matrimonial practice, but does not affect the main dramatic point. The essential fact is that Claudio is, and must be, caught in an ambiguous situation in order for the conflict between Angelo and Isabella to take place. The ambiguity of the offence is heightened by the way Shakespeare introduces Claudio. His arrest is announced successively by a madam and a bawd, his part is taken by the loose-talking Lucio, and Lucio insists on calling his offence lechery. In this manner Shakespeare creates a sordid background for Claudio's crime, and though Claudio explains himself, he does not dispel the cloud that hangs over his relations with Juliet. As Claudio himself admits, Juliet and he could not restrain their mutual entertainment when her dowry was withheld. In short, their love overwhelmed the need for restraint.

We might immediately note, with Clifford Leech,[17] that the lady's name seems to echo that other Juliet who, however, was able to restrain herself – at least, with a balcony for protection. If we consider the later Juliet further, we find that she is a unique figure in Shakespeare. For the most part, chastity characterizes Shakespeare's heroines. Setting aside prostitutes and adulteresses, such as Lady Faulconbridge in *King John*, we find that young, unmarried women who commit fornication are limited to Margaret in *Much Ado About Nothing*, Cressida, Antiochus' daughter, and this Juliet. Though Margaret is a wanton, her offence is circumstantial, being dependent on Borachio's reported use of her balcony rather

---

[16]Ernest Schanzer, "The Marriage-Contracts in *Measure for Measure*," *Shakespeare Survey 13* (1960), pp. 81-89; S. Nagarajan, "*Measure for Measure* and Elizabethan Betrothals," *Shakespeare Quarterly*, XIV (1963), 115-19.
[17]Clifford Leech, "The 'Meaning' of *Measure for Measure*," *Shakespeare Survey 3* (1950), p. 73.

than upon overt sexual transgression. Cressida is more clearly a wanton, well on the way to prostitution. Antiochus' daughter is an unnatural monster. Only Juliet is shown to be wholesome as well as unchaste. She – and Claudio – were undoubtedly motivated by deep passion just as Vico, the Claudio figure in Giraldi Cinthio's novella, "The Story of Epitia," upon which the play is ultimately based, was also strongly moved by "the violent impulse that Love had in his heart."[18] Legally Claudio is being punished for fornication but in truth for having loved deeply and immoderately. This passion, however, is hinted not shown, and should lead us to consider the place of passion in *Measure for Measure*. We have seen how central it is to the dramatic development of a tragedy. How does it manifest itself in this work?

Comment by other characters as well as illustration by his own behaviour amply establishes Angelo as a severely restrained, cold, and passionless individual. Isabella is likewise restrained, or perhaps the better term should be inhibited. The Duke, though not as cold-natured as they, is reserved. As he hastens to assure Friar Thomas,

> Believe not that the dribbling dart of love
> Can pierce a complete bosom. (I. ii. 2-3)

Thus, the three major figures of the play eschew the passion that has overwhelmed Claudio and Juliet. As a result they are ill prepared to judge the delinquent couple. Their denial of love does not ban passion from the play, however. Instead, it leads to another sort of peculiar and powerful passion that accompanies the action. It is a punitive passion that guides all three. How that punitive passion ultimately yields to a more healthy and balanced affection can be traced through the action.

The verse and tone of the first scene are measured and restrained. All emotional expression is tempered. The Duke wants no ceremony on his departure. He entrusts "mortality and mercy" to live in Angelo's "tongue, and heart," an odd expectation of one so self-controlled. He departs, affecting love for the people but deploring any effort they may make to manifest their affection in "loud applause and *Aves* vehement" (70).

[18]Giraldi Cinthio, *Hecatommithi*, as printed in Geoffrey Bullough, *Narrative and Dramatic Sources of Shakespeare*, vol. II (London and New York: Routledge and Kegan Paul and Columbia University Press, 1958), p. 422.

In Act I, scene ii lust and passion are interwoven. Claudio represents the kind of transgressor whom the new deputy is determined to squash. He stands for true but immoderate love. In the next scene the Duke rejects the idea that love could have led him to seek a disguise of Friar Thomas. During the course of his explanation to the Friar, he contrasts Angelo's firm and dispassioned temper with the record of his own indulgent toleration of behaviour of which he disapproved. His recital is a self-indictment that does not oppose warmth to coldness but a tepid acceptance to a moral rigour.

In Act I, scene iv Isabella is introduced as a female counterpart to Angelo. The Duke has just described Angelo as a man who "scarce confesses / That his blood flows; or that his appetite / Is more to bread than stone" (I.iii.51-53); Isabella at once appears, not as contrast, but as parallel, desiring more restraints. She has deliberately joined a strict order of nuns which severely limits communication with men, thus ruling out the possibility that "the dribbling dart of love" could ever strike. Her powers are mental rather than physical, as we are advised by Claudio. In an earlier scene he told Lucio that

> in her youth
> There is a prone and speechless dialect
> Such as move men. (I. ii. 172-74)

Although this speech is often cited as referring specifically to Isabella, it is actually applicable to youth in general. Claudio says, in effect, that Isabella is still quite young, and shares with youth a capacity to touch men's hearts. Her particular attribute is less common, for in addition to her youth,

> she hath prosperous art
> When she will play with reason and discourse,
> And well she can persuade. (I. ii. 174-76)

In this same scene that we first meet Isabella (I.iv), Lucio reiterates the Duke's description of Angelo's coldness, "a man whose blood / Is very snow-broth" (57-58). He never feels the "wanton stings and motions of the sense; / But doth rebate and blunt his natural edge / With profits of the mind, study and fast" (59-61). This portrait can be equally applied to Isabella. Up to this scene then, a glimmer of deep-felt passion is revealed in Claudio, a lusty pseudo-passion in Lucio, austerity in the Duke, and asceticism in Isabella and Angelo. The interchange among characters has also been reserved except for Claudio's plea to Lucio. I would further suggest that Lucio's mocking approach to Isabella is not only an expression of his character but a deliberate effort by Shakespeare to keep the scene cool.

During the interrogation of Act II, scene i Angelo illustrates the coldness of which we have heard, and Escalus shows the same sort of tolerance that the Duke seeks to extirpate. Restraint in the guise of Elbow is silly, and bawdy wisdom has the better not only of him but of Escalus. Once again liberty is counselled and once again liberty replies to the counsel: "I shall follow it as the flesh and fortune shall better determine" (250-51). Through this scene the rich warmth of human feeling, whether the anguish of Hamlet or the deep yearning of Viola, is barely evident. It is in Act II, scene ii that passion makes its appearance.

For the meeting of Angelo and Isabella, Shakespeare carefully prepares the dramatic ground. He brings together two supposedly cold natures, the first dedicated to rigour, the other inclined to "reason and discourse" though called upon to "weep and kneel." Isabella begins her plea for Claudio's life by playing nicely upon her moral attitude and her sisterly compulsion. The substance of the debate is the counterclaims of mercy and justice as well as the dangers of overweening authority. But this is merely the raw material of the interchange. It is quite evident that Angelo is moved not by Isabella's argument but by her eloquent passion. The manner not the content affects him. To make this unmistakable Shakespeare places both Lucio and the Provost in the scene. Our appreciation of the rising heat of the action can be better gained by following their remarks rather than Isabella's plea. After himself failing to win pardon for Claudio, the Provost prays that "Heaven [will] give [Isabella] moving graces!" (36) – that is, power to stir emotion in Angelo. His wish comes true, but not in the sense he intended. After Isabella's introductory statements, when she is ready to accept Angelo's rebuff, Lucio admonishes her to "entreat him, / Kneel down before him, hang upon his gown" (43-45) – in short, use emotion not words. "You are too cold." "Cold," the very term applied to Angelo so often, whose "blood is very snow-broth." She returns to her plea, but several speeches later Lucio again scolds her, "You are too cold." Shortly thereafter Isabella warms to her task, for fourteen lines later Lucio tells her, "Ay, touch him: there's the vein" (70).

But what is it in her appeal that begins to touch Angelo at this moment? Isabella has argued that if roles had been reversed, had he and Claudio or he and Isabella been in opposite circumstances, they would not have shown such sternness. While this may be so for Claudio, what we know now and later learn of Isabella makes this latter claim far-fetched. In any case her argument is identical to one urged the scene before by Escalus (II.i.8-16). Its repetition is not designed to reveal Isabella's wisdom but her ability to take a conventional plea and fill it with passion. Lucio's next echo is more approving. "Ay, well said," he comments after Isabella's cry for mercy culminates in the plea:

> Good, good my lord, bethink you:
> Who is it that hath died for this offence?
> There's many have committed it. (II. ii. 88-90)

This is virtually identical with the Provost's words at the beginning of the scene:

> Alas,
> He hath but as offended in a dream;
> All sects, all ages smack of this vice, and he
> To die for't! (II. ii. 3-6)

Again, it is not the idea, which we have already encountered, but the passion Isabella brings to the idea that begins to touch Angelo. At this point Angelo makes his lengthiest and most eloquent defence that he punishes one to save many. In the face of this argument Isabella changes her tactic and attacks authority when it fully uses its full power. "That's well said," again chimes Lucio. The rhythm of the verse, the choral cheers of Lucio and the Provost, and Angelo's defensive remarks all combine to heighten the emotional climate of the scene, in effect, for the first time in the play. Isabella fairly sings: "Could great men thunder / As Jove himself does . . . thunder; nothing but thunder . . . But man, proud man . . . Plays such fantastic tricks before high heaven / As makes the angels weep. . . ." (111 ff.) Isabella's oration, seconded and intermixed with Lucio's encouragement and the Provost's prayer (the first time Lucio and the Provost echo each other) reaches a pitch in the repetition of an idea we have heard expressed previously by Escalus and Isabella: "Go to your bosom, / Knock there, and ask your heart what it doth know / That's like my brother's fault" (137-39). Isabella disconcerts Angelo. He utters his first aside:

Bernard Beckerman

> She speaks, and 'tis such sense
> That my sense breeds with it. (142-43)

Sense! We have heard that word applied to Angelo before. Lucio told Isabella that Angelo

> never feels
> The wanton stings and motions of the sense, (I. iv. 58-59)

and here we see him feel these stings and motions, so much so that he is driven to flee Isabella's presence. At this juncture, when Angelo is most vulnerable, experiencing an unfamiliar temptation, desperate to escape from her overpowering passion, Isabella utters fateful words that introduce an alien and dishonourable thought:

> Gentle my lord, turn back ...
> Hark, how I'll bribe you: good my lord, turn back.
>
> (II. ii. 144-46)

Her bribe, she explains, is prayer. But at that moment he heard nothing but the ring of illicit appeal. Babes in the giving and taking of passion, they do not know when to cease or how to respond. Isabella desperately utters the word "bribe" because she fails to perceive the effect she is having on Angelo. Angelo, feeling guilty already about the welling of sensation within himself, is ready to believe that something wrong lurks in her plea. And what has been the substance of her plea? Fundamentally, it is not based on the preeminence of mercy but on the chastisement of man. She can warm to the subject of deriding "proud man." And he, who has been adamant to her reason, responds to her scorn.

His soliloquy that follows her exit is reactive, during which he tries to understand the nature and responsibility of the feeling that has been stirred within him. He is fearful of the direction towards which his thoughts tend: "What, do I love her ... What is't I dream on?" His temper is stirred, with frightening effects. Thus, in the course of the scene, passion of a tragedic dimension bursts forth. The sentiments of mercy and humility that accompany this impassioned outburst have universal appeal so that our sympathy lies with Isabella. We are moved, however, less by her as a thinker and more by the passion that invests the sentiments. Her speeches are rousing and so they rouse us. To say, as Bennett and Stevenson do,[19] that we maintain a detached interest in the scene neglects

[19]Bennett, p. 158; Stevenson, p. 18.

the high emotion called for by Lucio and the obvious power that Isabella musters. We have thus reached one plateau of passion as a foreshadowing for others to follow.

Before the second meeting of Angelo and Isabella the brief confessional scene between the Duke and Juliet takes place. The dominant mood of that scene, though low-keyed, is contrite love. Juliet's sincerity is affirmed by her simple interruption of the Duke's rather laborious teaching. Of her sin, she says:

> I do repent me as it is an evil,
> And take the shame with joy. (II. iii. 35-36)

Her emotional state as well as her deep loyalty is a measure against which other behaviour can be judged.

As Angelo waits for Isabella's second visit (II.iv), he is distracted by his remembrance of her. He cannot concentrate upon his prayers, feeling that all he has valued is no more than "an idle plume / Which the air beats for vain." Dramatically, what happens is not that Angelo works out his confusion in self-argument, but that in musing over his distraction, he is overwhelmed by unaccustomed passion. Suddenly, he who hardly confesses "that his blood flows" cries out, "Blood, thou art blood," as he feels the inner surge of feeling. He experiences in actuality what Escalus hypothesized: "The resolute acting of [his] blood" (II.i.12). Isabella is announced. His body shakes:

> O heavens,
> Why does my blood thus muster to my heart,
> Making both it unable for itself,
> And dispossessing all my other parts
> Of necessary fitness? (II. iv. 19-23)

Thus, instead of being wholly a hypocrite who prepares to face the sainted Isabella, as some have charged, Angelo is a man unsettled, unable to act with his usual gravity, unprepared for the wracking passions that beset him. It is in this divided state that he encounters Isabella once again.

As I read the scene, their meeting progresses in three segments. It is Angelo who carries the action forward. Ostensibly he must give Isabella an answer to her plea for Claudio's life. In truth, he must find a way to express his new-found passion. Keeping in mind his divided state, we note that he plays with words, that his approach is circuitous, posing as he does hypothetical possibilities. His inner turmoil is revealed in a spontaneous cry, "Ha! fie, these filthy vices!" He seizes on Isabella's admission that one can separate heaven's law from earth's law to argue that a compelled sin is not sin at all, but immediately argues against that remark, "for I can speak / Against the thing I say." The more he systematically, almost legalistically, endeavours to convey his desire to Isabella, the more is the gap between her understanding and his. He accuses her of deception, and finally once again systematically, though hypothetically, poses the choice between her body and her brother's life. Through this first segment, Angelo has conquered his agitation sufficiently to bring his desire to a veiled revelation. When Isabella refuses to choose sin for life, he asserts that Claudio must die and she accepts the decision. The first segment ends.

The next stage of development has a far more personal tone. The speech is conversational, the style less hortatory. No longer does Angelo pursue his goal, but instead the two converse about human frailty. Isabella even confesses to sharing the frailty of women. Her attitude towards men is evident in her admission:

> Women? – Help, heaven! Men their creation mar
> In profiting by them. (II. iv. 126-27)

And how can we blame her? The women of the play are either victims of men (Mariana and Juliet) or panders to them (Mrs. Overdone). Angelo takes up Isabella's confession by *pleading*, not demanding, that she be the woman that is natural to her. The intimate passion of his words is apparent in her request that he "speak the former language." He reveals his love. Whether or not his statement, "Plainly conceive, I love you" means "I lust for you" or "I love you physically and spiritually," we do not know. There is no question, however, that Angelo here again is most vulnerable. He has exposed his deepest emotions plaintively. There is even something pathetic in his promise to Isabella that Claudio will not die if she gives him love. I am well aware that these lines have often been delivered in a peremptory and tyrannical manner and that a case can be made for treating them as naked threats. But to do so belies the initial disturbed state of Angelo, the impersonal manner of his earlier arguments, and the change of tone in segment two. I do not wish to suggest that Angelo is offering Isabella an untainted love, but that his passion is untutored, and therefore responsive to circumstances. Unfortunately, Isabella is one least capable of deal-ing with a passion that Angelo calls "the strong and swelling evil / Of [his] conception" (6-7). She begins the last segment of the scene by threatening to expose Angelo unless he grants Claudio pardon. In effect, she attempts to blackmail him. The result instead is that she releases all his inhibitions. Whatever guilty restraint he has exercised vanishes as he gives his "sensual race the rein" (159). In an instant all the evil passion of his heart pours forth, raising the scene to an intense pitch and leaving Isabella shattered and forlorn, free only to tell Claudio the truth and prepare him for death.

While Isabella is on her way to the prison, the Duke is comfort-ing Claudio, if urging him to discard life as worthless can be called comforting. His speech tempers the high emotion of the scene that has preceded and of the action that is about to follow.

Isabella arrives. The Provost secretes the disguised Duke where he may listen to the visitation of sister to brother, and the action proceeds to a final plateau of intensity. Isabella reveals Angelo's request. Claudio is appalled, but then reverses himself. In contrast to the Duke's measured reasoning on death, Claudio becomes hysterical as he contemplates his execution and cries out, "Sweet sister, let me live." She, revolted by his weakness, explodes in a vituperative attack upon her brother, reaching a pitch of emotion not hitherto witnessed and not heard in the play again. Once more, we see her passion revealed through an attack upon a faithless man.

The heightening of passion that I have been describing in the first half of *Measure for Measure* follows the same pattern as that in the tragedies. A sequence of confrontations arising from an initial precipitating contrast produces strong reactive outbursts. Each outburst is composed of threat and castigation in differing proportions. Each is, to some extent, sadistic, the final outburst of Isabella against Claudio most evidently so. By the time the action reaches its fullest elaboration, we have become alienated from Isabella. Whetstone in *Promos and Cassandra* showed that Cas-sandra's sacrifice of her body to save her brother leads not to damnation but to redemption of the seducer, Promos, and her sub-sequent marriage to him. Shakespeare reveals what might happen if chastity is defended to the death. It becomes vain and perverted. Not content merely to deny Claudio's request for life, Isabella heaps abuse upon him, and at the peak of her rage violates her very calling.

> I'll pray a thousand prayers for thy death;
> No word to save thee. (III. i. 145-46)

Though the action during this first half of the play is tinged with irony and shot through with low comedy, the dominant strain is serious, and the issues mortal. It is at this point that the narrative split occurs and the dramatic tone changes.

The change is immediate and thoroughgoing, as we have already seen. Poetry gives way to prose, passion to intrigue, tragedy to ironic comedy. The mode of the second half is designed to cleanse the perverted passions of the first. Through much of the second half passion is by-passed or curtailed. For example, in the latter part of Act III, scene i the Duke describes Mariana as having been left in tears. Angelo's unkindness to her, instead of quenching her love, "hath, like an impediment in the current, made it more violent and unruly" (242-43). Yet when we first meet Mariana she is listening to a melancholy song, and though she refers to her "brawling discontent," Shakespeare does not choose to show it to us. Another type of by-pass occurs in Act IV, scene iii, when the Duke informs Isabella of her brother's death. Here Shakespeare chooses to give her three brief lines: one of rage against Angelo, and two of conventional lament:

> Unhappy Claudio! wretched Isabel!
> Injurious world! most damned Angelo! (IV. iii. 121-22)

A personal lament for Claudio is spoken, ironically enough, by Lucio. He offers Isabella his condolences. Though his remarks do have a touch of mockery about them, his oath, "By my troth, Isabel, I loved thy brother" (155), seems sincere enough, and one of the rare expressions of genuine emotion in the third and fourth acts.

The clue to the second half of the play is, of course, the Duke. Lucio, the slanderer, says, in commenting on Claudio's sentence, that "The Duke . . . would have dark deeds darkly answered: he would never bring them to light" (III.ii.170-72). Are we to take this slanderer's word as gospel? When we overview the Duke, we see indeed that he has preferred the dark answer. He chose to leave Angelo behind while he lurked about beholding his deputy's sway. He does not like "to stage [himself] to the [people's] eyes" (I.i.68); he spies on his subjects; he intrigues to save Claudio. In all this he shows a propensity for covert action until he resolves, departing from Lucio's characterization of him, to discover all in the final act.

Throughout his intrigue the Duke exhibits intense emotion principally – and this is significant – in his response to Lucio's slander. It is at such moments that poetry reappears. After his first encounter with Lucio, he comments:

> No might nor greatness in mortality
> Can censure 'scape. Back-wounding calumny
> The whitest virtue strikes. What king so strong
> Can tie the gall up in the slanderous tongue? (III. ii. 179-82)

He repeats this idea in Act IV, scene i (60-65). Some editors claim that this latter passage was originally a continuance of the passage just quoted. I do not have the time to argue this point textually, but the dramatic evidence is that the duplication is intentional. The Duke is stung by Lucio's slander, however fanciful it may be, and cannot forget it. Only reluctantly and at the very last does he pardon Lucio. These responses to slander, which involve the Duke's public image, may be contrasted with the Duke's reaction to Angelo's duplicity. His anger is genuine enough, but Shakespeare casts it in a rhyming tetrameter that has the effect of undercutting the emotional turbulence of the passage (III.ii.254-75).

In Acts III and IV only two relationships carry genuine dramatic force: the Duke's two interchanges with Lucio and his single exchange with Barnardine. In the interchanges with Lucio the Duke encounters liberty in the guise of slander; through the exchange with Barnardine he faces the consequences of his procrastination in meting out justice. Lucio and Barnardine each embody defiance of established order in a comic, almost surrealistic manner. The Duke's passionate utterances against them underscore his lack of dexterity in warding off their thrusts. Despite our knowledge that Lucio's sallies will revert against him, we are delighted by his outrageous lies, for through them we are able to witness the discomfiture of the Duke who, having struggled to remain unsullied by the pollution of libertinism, is soiled in such an irresponsible, yet merry manner. These encounters educate the Duke. Through them he undergoes a purgatorial process: his vanity is traduced and his most awesome power, the capacity to deal death, is contemptuously dismissed. In contrast to these challenges, his scheming seems efficient but beside the point. Only when he brings matters to light in the fifth act does he effectively deal with the consequences of his past delinquency. The horror at the corruption he found in Vienna, asserted just before he is unmasked by Lucio, is essentially an expression of self-condemnation (I.i.314-20).

Shakespeare dramatizes the changes that take place within the Duke through the elaborate arrangement that the Duke makes for staging himself to the people's eyes. This finale of discovery is painstakingly worked out, and even the New Cambridge editors who see much revision in the text admit that the last scene is all of a piece. Highly schematic, the finale unfolds beautifully. The audience is privy to all the essential facts: the Duke's disguise, the preservation of Claudio, and the true lover of Angelo. It can thus devote its attention to two related sequences: (1) how the characters other than the Duke react to the successive revelations, and (2) how the Duke handles the revelations themselves.

First, let us consider the nature and focus of the reactions. In most instances they are not expressed through what the characters say but through the Duke's recognition of the reactions. The reactions themselves are perfunctory. To the most momentous revelation of the scene, the unmasking of the Duke-Friar, Lucio has a single-line reaction, Angelo an eight-line speech of submission, Escalus a line and a half of surprise, and Isabella two lines of apology. By the time Claudio is returned to her, she is mute. Throughout, Shakespeare seems to de-emphasize character reactions deliberately. For what reason? I think his purpose can be most clearly discerned in the way he handles the accusation against Angelo.

When Isabella first attempts to address the returning Duke, Angelo tries to prevent her from obtaining a hearing. He accuses her of lacking firm wits. She will speak "most bitterly and strange" because her brother died by course of justice. But when Isabella actually makes her accusation, Angelo does not speak. The exchange remains between her and the Duke except for Lucio's interjections that provoke the Duke's acid rejoinders. At one point the Duke suggests a possible reaction for Angelo. "Do you not smile at this, Lord Angelo?" (165). Angelo does not answer. Only when Mariana accuses him of having been in her arms, does he respond in a puzzled manner and ask to see her face. He defends himself against her accusation and then, revealing that he has taken the Duke's clue by saying "I did but smile till now" (232), he asks the right to judge the two women. During this portion of the hearing Angelo has, for the most part, been kept in the background. He is given little opportunity to reveal his emotional state. He smiles, but that is a conventional expression of villainy, and surely serves as a mask here.

It is after Angelo asks to judge the women that Shakespeare's intention becomes even more obvious. Despite his request and the Duke's assent, Angelo is not the one to investigate the charges. Instead, it is Escalus who takes the lead. The purpose is to keep attention off Angelo and on the Duke, for Escalus says of Isabel, "I will go darkly to work with her" (277). In taking this tack, he is a throwback to the Duke who would have dark things darkly answered.

This discussion brings us to the second sequence: how the Duke handles the revelations. Throughout the finale the Duke retains firm hold of the action, so firmly that it has given rise to the theory that the finale enacts the revelation of Divine Power. Escalus, as substitute Duke in the passage just cited, suggests the Duke investigating himself. In the course of the play the Duke passes from working darkly to staging himself to the people's eyes and through doing so comes to terms with law and order. In the last act he commences by purporting to render justice and finally renders mercy, starting sternly, and then proceeding to leniency, first with Angelo and then with Lucio. His final leniency with Lucio returns the situation to the beginning of the play: a man is charged with fornication with a woman to whom he has promised marriage. The action retrogresses a step further when the Duke pardons this liberty. The effect is complex. The form seems cyclical. The old tolerance seems to have reasserted itself. But perhaps the worst excesses will be avoided, for liberty has been replaced by holy matrimony. True, virtually all the marriages that end this peculiar comedy are tainted: Claudio and Juliet's, Angelo and Mariana's and Lucio and Kate Keepdown's. Of the impending marriage of the Duke and Isabella, little can be predicted. It certainly is not a conventional joining of sovereign and beloved such as *Twelfth Night* illustrates. The form of comedy completes the work, but the impression of quizzical irony remains behind.

To my mind, the dramaturgic evidence that Shakespeare composed *Measure for Measure* with great care is overwhelming. Yet the play is still, in J. W. Lever's words, a "flawed masterpiece."[20]

[20]J. W. Lever, Introduction to *Measure for Measure* (new Arden edition, 1965), p. xcvii.

Its failings are most apparent in the second half. They are not a consequence, however, of Shakespeare's supposedly "flagging skill" as a poet, as Pater seems to suggest. That the poetry of Acts IV and V does not have the power of the second act poetry is obvious enough. But I don't think Shakespeare intended it to have that power. Nor are the play's flaws due to the distasteful participation of Isabella in the bed trick. The flaws, as Quiller-Couch asserts, are aesthetic, though again, not because Shakespeare failed to maintain adequate inspiration for the creation of conventional tragedy or comedy. Instead, he sought to create a peculiar type of tragi-comedy. The intrigue of the second half, essentially comedic, was designed to purge the essentially tragic passion of the first. The aesthetic fault is that there are too many passages solely devoted to the exposition of plots and schemes. Unhappily, exposition of this kind is virtually impossible to make interesting unless a passion for revenge informs it. But *Measure for Measure* is not a revenge play, and the Duke is not a revenge figure. He is a conniver with moral aims. Shakespeare endows him neither with the loathing for humanity characteristic of Vindice in *The Revenger's Tragedy* nor with the satiric misanthropy affected by Macilente in *Every Man Out of His Humour*. As a result, except for his encounters with Lucio and Barnardine, the Duke fails to display a distinctive temperament in the third and fourth acts. In addition, the Duke's plotting utilizes Isabella but does not advance her, requires new characters such as Mariana, Abhorson, and Barnardine, but does not allow them scope to function, penetrates the purgatorial recesses of the prison, but does not fully exploit its potential grotesquerie. By being completely in the hands of the all-seeing and all-powerful Duke, the intrigue leaves little room for passion or complication. Yet the intrigue must be in the Duke's hands, for he must teach himself. Unfortunately, this form of plotting did not permit Shakespeare's enormous powers adequate opportunity for elaboration.

Why Shakespeare chose so uncongenial a plot is puzzling. His care in constructing the play rules out the explanation that haste or disinterestedness led him to scant his efforts. Perhaps he was attracted by the fashion for disguised rulers as portrayed in such a work as John Marston's *The Malcontent*, a play that he and his fellow actors "liberated" from the repertory of the Children of the Queen's Revels. In this kind of plot he may have seen dramatic possibilities for tonal contrast that, unfortunately, he was unable to realize. Wholehearted as his effort was, the disguise device proved intractable for his purposes and thus contributed to a partial failure.

This failure, however, is not beyond theatrical remedy. After all, the play contains two of the most powerful scenes in the Shakespearean canon. It also embodies the dark sense of man's psychic frailties. And it culminates in a *tour de force* of discovery that is both a theatrical delight and an object lesson. By correctly identifying the weaknesses and by deeply appreciating Shakespeare's artistic intent, we can better place both halves of the play in proper dramatic balance and find those stage moments that will fulfill Shakespeare's experiment in tragicomedy.

Marry, Sweet Wag

PETER DAVISON

I had been invited to wind up the International Shakespeare Conference with a short talk at once light and serious. I decided to speak – indeed, to perform and even sing – Shakespearean burlesque to meet the requirement of "the light" and then to turn, perhaps too dramatically, to what, for all its brilliance, seemed to me to be a form of academic burlesque – at least, to the extent of its imitation, if unwitting, of what it condemned. It is this second, more serious, part of what I said that is reprinted here.

The first article in the 1969 issue of *Studies in Bibliography* (XXII) was a long and thorough critique of current bibliographic practice. It was called "Printers of the Mind: Some Notes on Bibliographical Theories and Printing-House Practices," and was written by Dr. D. F. McKenzie. The validity of individual points and the brilliance of the approach carried, it seemed to me, a conviction which detailed study of the article did not warrant. Despite its many qualities it appeared to be based on a misunderstanding of the nature of humanistic enquiry, to confuse this with science, to recognize but one kind of science and to argue fallaciously for an approach (the hypothetico-deductive method) as being singularly suited to science and to bibliography. These misconceptions have serious, and perhaps unfortunate, implications.

Dr. McKenzie began by arguing that bibliographers must proceed by the hypothetic deductive method; then, basing what he said on his own study of printing at the Cambridge University Press between 1696 and 1712, and on the work of two eighteenth-century printers, Charles Ackers and William Bowyer (whose ledger is as yet unpublished, but of which extracts were given in the appendices to the article), he considered problems such as workmen's output, edition sizes, and the relationship of composition to presswork. He then attacked current theories of compositors' measures, cast-off copy, skeleton formes, proof correction, and press figures. Finally he argued that bibliographers ought to show a greater concern for historical perspective.

In my after-dinner talk I could only touch on a few of the points made by Dr. McKenzie. I hoped to do no more than prompt a certain caution in accepting what he said *tout court* until an opportunity arose when I could analyse in detail the implications of what he had to say. It is thus only the simpler and more obvious aspects that are touched on here. I have left until another occasion a discussion of the shortcomings of the hypothetico-deductive method when applied in textual studies, and of the much misunderstood relationship of bibliography and the editorial process to science.

To consider such a sustained and intelligent attack as Dr. McKenzie's in the same light as the burlesques I have so far mentioned is to seem slighting in a way I do not intend. This article is so good, particularly in what it has to say about the use by bibliographers of inductive argument, so convincing in its horrendous collection of bibliographers' sins of omission and commission, so full of necessary, intelligent, and perceptive warnings, that it is almost impertinent to raise even the merest quibble – especially in the face of the warm approval accorded Dr. McKenzie's article by the *TLS* (22 May 1969). Yet, serious in tone and implications though Dr. McKenzie's article is, in its conclusion that we should abandon analytic bibliography and devote all our attention to enumerative bibliography, we come near to a burlesque of our subject and, indeed, of man's urge to inquire. And perhaps one might even argue unintentional burlesque in that Dr. McKenzie, despite being so consistently brilliant, slips into a form of burlesque in imitating, doubtless unwittingly, what he describes.

It is not difficult to add to the chamber of horrors which Dr. McKenzie parades before us (and which Professor Fredson Bowers, frequently the object of attack, so generously publishes). Thus, Professor Bowers himself, in discussing *Romeo and Juliet*, Q2, suggests that Lady Capulet's speech prefixes generally follow the pattern described for her husband.[1] This is not so. Up to and including H2r (III.iii) Father Capulet has 12 speeches in 2 forms (*Capu* 10; *Cap* 2); his wife has 14 speeches in 5 forms (*Wife* 5; *Old*

[1] *Textual and Literary Criticism* (Cambridge, 1959), p. 88.

La 6; *Mo* 1; *Capu Wi* 1; *Ca W* 1). Thereafter the husband has 35 speeches with 6 forms of prefix (*Ca* 18; *Fa* 11; *Cap* 3; *Capu* 1; *Capel* 1; *Fat* 1), whereas his wife has over twice as many speeches as before (31) but still in no more than 5 forms (*La* 13; *Mo* 11; *M* 4; *Wife* 2; *Wi* 1; the *M* at II.v.15 is disregarded).

More serious is Professor Bowers's unqualified approval of Paul Maas's approach to stemmatics. In the light of the work of George Thomson on Aeschylus and George Kane on Piers Plowman A, can one happily accept the suggestion on the first page of *Bibliography and Textual Criticism*[2] that the general principles for dealing with manuscript traditions have been formulated for some years and can be found conveniently summarized in Maas's *Textual Criticism?*

But Dr. McKenzie goes much further than picking little holes such as these, and he is so convincing that to the *TLS* reviewer he seems, for example, to have demolished the greater part of the theory of skeleton formes. But is the situation *quite* like this? Undoubtedly Dr. McKenzie exposes many errors and shows how often conjecture becomes fact in the mind of the bibliographer. For this salutary reminder we must be grateful – it is well merited – but to speak of demolishing the greater part of the theory of skeleton formes or to go on to suggest the abandonment of analytic bibliography is, I suggest, a burlesque of the actual situation.

If we look as closely at Dr. McKenzie's article as it deserves, we may find the situation less hopeless than he or the *TLS* reviewer suggest and, indeed, that he himself does what he rightly condemns bibliographers for doing.

Dr. McKenzie percipiently questions the arguments for close relationships of composition and presswork, and in particular he shows that "the fine considerations of timing implied by many studies devoted to the analysis of a single work may be a world away from the reality." (*S.B.* XXII, 18 [page numbers only given hereafter]). This, he argues, is because we usually study the production of only a single book at one time, whereas *all* books published about such a time ought to be examined in order that we can take due account of concurrent printing. (This does seem to assume that we have, or at least know, of all these books – a situation unhappily not obtaining.) One must also, he points out, be aware that workmen now, and those living before the Industrial Revolution, had very different attitudes to work, and he quotes Sir
[2]Oxford, 1964.

William Temple to the effect that the mass of labourers worked only to relieve present want (p. 10). He argues that we are wrong to assume "that an economic relationship between composition and presswork is necessary on any *one* book for the business as a whole to be successful" (p. 17). All this, surely, suggests that we must be more thorough and more cautious.

Despite the intelligence of his strictures, it is just here that I would begin to quibble. When Dr. McKenzie suggests that a phrase used by Professor Bowers, "the press was idle," is misleading, he has a point; but so may Dr. McKenzie be misleading. "Under the conditions of concurrent printing the press would not be 'idle' at all," he argues, "but employed on another book" (p. 24). How does Dr. McKenzie know this? A small job, possibly, but a book? Does that not argue for rather a high degree of organization and method – a plan for the continuous working of the press and the provision of appropriately damped paper – which is denied by Dr. McKenzie's own argument for the disinterestedness of the pre-Industrial Revolution worker in flat-out, full-time work? In view of his own argument, ought he not simply to regard the press as idle?

But this is a minor quibble. What seems to me more serious is the assumption that we have two kinds of worker – pre- and post-Industrial Revolution man. But was the sixteenth-century workman as unwilling to work regularly as Dr. McKenzie's Cambridge printers of the early eighteenth century? To what extent had the old guild relationship of master and man carried on into the sixteenth century? Doubtless the relationship is idealized by Dekker in *The Shoemaker's Holiday*, but can one wholly disregard the influence of the guild tradition and still claim "historical perspective"? Is it enough to suggest that "one of the reasons why Elizabethan printers tried so often to exceed their allowed number of apprentices *may* [my stress] have been that apprentices could be commanded to work regularly where journeymen could not" (p. 11). In his footnote to this passage I cannot help but wonder if Dr. McKenzie is not doing what he rightly accuses bibliographers of doing – generalizing from an instance (in this case the litigation in 1592 involving Benjamin Prince and John Legate). I sense that historical perspective is here being used rather loosely.

Dr. McKenzie sets his argument in a context of employees' attitudes. But what of the employers? Might not they be concerned to evolve a more systematic approach to their work, especially at this time of the rise of capitalism? Dr. McKenzie delightfully quotes from *Daniel Deronda*. Perhaps I can quote from another work of fiction, *The Shoemaker's Holiday*.[3] You will all recall the urgency with which Simon Eyre presses his household, workmen and family, in order to get them all working well before breakfast, in Act I, scene iv: "O haste to worke my fine foreman, haste to worke ... to worke, to worke a while, and then to breakfast" (11. 22 and 113-14). But even more significant is the way in which his former foreman, Hodge, imitates him when he becomes a master: "plie your worke to day, we loytred yesterday [the occasion of celebrating Eyre's election], to it pell mel, that may liue to be Lord Maiors, or Alderman at least" (IV. i. 2-4). And he is just as keen to have his men working before breakfast as was Simon Eyre. Of course, *The Shoemaker's Holiday* is not a social treatise, but that urgency is not, perhaps, entirely without warrant. Employers of any age are likely to be interested in efficiency, especially in a relatively new trade. I find it difficult to believe that Medieval and Tudor man was quite unmethodical. One has only to imagine many piles of drying, damped paper cluttering up a pressroom to wonder whether *some* sort of order might not have been *aimed* at in the Elizabethan printing house.

Recently I was examining Peter Short's edition of *1 Henry IV* for my forthcoming edition in the *New Penguin Shakespeare*, and I looked at a number of other books he was then printing (though not, I regret, to establish a scheme of concurrent printing). I looked in detail at the other plays he printed: *The taming of a Shrew*, 1594 and 1596; Garnier's *The tragedie of Antonie* and another octavo of 1595, *The true tragedie of Richard Duke of Yorke*; and *Arden of Feversham*, 1592, which is possibly his. For each of these plays a single skeleton forme was used – a trifle surprising in a prominent printer of this time if bibliographers' ideas are anything to go by, that such a technique was wasteful of time and thus passing out of use. When I looked at *1 Henry IV*, Q1, I found that though *two* skeleton formes were used, they were arranged as if a *pair of single skeleton formes* were being employed. (That is, one forme, instead of being used for all inners, was used for both inners and outers of alternate gatherings.) Now whatever

[3]*The Dramatic Works of Thomas Dekker*, ed. Fredson Bowers (Cambridge, 1953), I.

specific conclusions may be drawn from this (and I may well have drawn the wrong ones), there is a general conclusion that seems to me relevant anent Dr. McKenzie's arguments. Am I wrong in imagining that however idle were Peter Short's workers (for which I have no evidence except what may be attributed to them by the process of historical perspective that they were of the species Pre-Industrial Revolution Man), there were signs of planned production? If this trifle of evidence about the use of skeleton formes in Peter Short's house is of any service, it is not, as Dr. McKenzie might suggest, that it destroys all faith in skeleton formes as evidence, but rather that it may modify, if ever so slightly, our understanding of the method of work in an Elizabethan printing house. Dr. McKenzie offers much evidence to suggest that our assumptions have been erroneous, but that is not in this case the same as demolishing the usefulness of this kind of investigation.

I referred to Dr. McKenzie's excellent argument regarding concurrent printing. This does not of itself deny a relationship of some kind between the work done, the compositor, and the pressman – though it is, as Dr. McKenzie rightly indicates, more complex than we may have imagined. Although Dr. McKenzie, in his study of printing at the Cambridge University Press between 1696 and 1712, shows "it was by no means rare at Cambridge for a compositor to have a monopoly on any one book, the work was usually shared" (p. 18). His analysis of work at Cambridge undermines the easy assumption of a work being set and run off by a small team.

I am not sure how far one is justified in transferring this evidence of university printing at Cambridge to commercial printing in London in the sixteenth century. Apart from differences in style and approach to that work, I have doubts for reasons of what might be called historical perspective in reverse. From 1949-1952 I worked for a small printer considerably less distinguished than the Cambridge University Press (or even perhaps than Peter Short). At that house it was the practice to allocate certain work to certain compositors (there were four in all, two on machines and two at the stone). Electoral registers were always set by one man; another set journals; the arrangement was varied only very rarely. There was certainly concurrent setting and much job work (an aspect about which in the sixteenth century, alas, we can know very little, and which Dr. McKenzie virtually disregards, seeing it simply as "this opportunistic resort to a theory of concurrent printing" which bibliographers employ to explain imbalances which they cannot otherwise account for [p. 35]). Despite the advances in technology (and this house though small was modern) there *was* a relationship between compositor and job and the reason for this became apparent to me when, later, I had to make use of trade setting. (There was no relation between compositor and pressman because jobs were allotted to the appropriate machine available.)

I do not argue that what happened in this small house in 1950 can be transferred to 1590; but I do wonder whether the practice may not be indicative of a relationship between man and job at least as worthy of consideration when we examine the sixteenth century as the examples of job-change reported by Dr. McKenzie from the eighteenth century.[4]

Furthermore, it is one thing to reproach bibliographers because "we have perhaps failed in our historical sense, too readily imputing our own twentieth-century ideas and interests and the assumptions of our own society – especially our economic assumptions – to men whose attitudes to work were quite different from ours" (p. 10), (does one here detect a conjecture edging into fact?) but it is quite another to give the impression that a full sense of historical perspective *can* be obtained. How difficult we have found it to recall exactly the social conditions of Shakespeare's time in order to aid our literary studies! Can we be any more hopeful in providing a full historical perspective for bibliographical studies? And if the perspective is not complete, what then? Abandon everything?

One can see how difficult it is to gain a full historical perspective by examining the evidence which Dr. McKenzie himself offers from Bowyer's printing house. Dr. McKenzie points out that "the *size* of 'Elizabethan' shops has perhaps been a little too readily set at one or two presses, and the 'strict limitation' on their numbers over-stressed" (p. 54). He argues very intelligently that they may

---

[4]*Monotype Newsletter* 86, December 1969, provides an interesting footnote to what I said at the Conference in July. An article on the *Pelican Shakespeare*, "Filmsetting the Bard," concludes: "The major task fell upon a team of two expert compositors, five other highly skilled technicians, one editorial reader, the typographer, and the General Editor. In *The Printing and Proof-Reading of the First Folio of Shakespeare* (Oxford, 1963), Professor Charlton Hinman identified four compositors and one apprentice who, in 1623, set the type for the first collected edition of Shakespeare's plays. *Plus ça change. . . .*" The last three words are those of the author of the article, not mine!

have been larger than we have imagined and then rests his argument by examining the implications of Elizabethan houses having only one or two presses.

> Grant for the moment that most Elizabethan shops were two-press and one-press houses; it may then be asked what the distribution of presses was within 18th-century houses. How many had two, how many had only one? In the second week of October 1732 even Bowyer had only two (See appendix II [f]). For the rest, no one knows, and even press figures may not tell us (p. 57).

Whether we can rely on historical perspective constructed from information which "even press figures may not tell us" seems a little doubtful. Nevertheless Dr. McKenzie's argument that Elizabethan houses may have been larger than we imagined is interesting. What, however, are we to make of the statement about Bowyer? The ledger recording work is not yet available to us so one can but rely on what Dr. McKenzie presents in his copious appendices. Table IIf for 8-14 October 1732 certainly shows two presses. The preceding table for 14-26 February 1732 shows five presses, however – nos 1, 2, 3, 5, and 7. What happened between February and October? Were three of these presses abandoned? Were *seven* presses available in February? Table IId for 31 Jan– 12 Feb 1732 shows only four presses – 1, 2, 3, and 7. Was Bowyer's then a four-press shop, but in the next week a five-press shop? Or really a seven-press shop all the time? When presses are not listed, did they cease to exist? Was there simply a lack of work, or are the records less complete than one imagines from their description? But in these circumstances can you really call this a two-press house on the strength of there being only two presses listed as working in one week? If a printer closes down for a week's holiday, does he become a no-press house? In a sense I suppose he does, but it is not really indicative of his printing practice.

When we look at the selection of case histories which Dr. Mc-Kenzie presents we do find a press number 4 although there is no sign of a press number 6. Was there no such press, or was it engaged on some unrecorded activity such as proofing – or even jobbing? If it was unrecorded, might there not also have been a press 8 or a press 9? I find it even more difficult to accept this argument that Bowyer's was a two-press house when I read Dr. McKenzie's account of the printing of Baxter's *Glossarium Anti-*

quitatum Britannicarum (pp. 71-72). Printing began one month after that two-press week in October and went on till June of the following year, 1733, and in all five presses were used.

I feel as much at a loss in gaining historical perspective from such evidence as Dr. McKenzie claims to do in understanding aspects of running-title analysis (p. 24). As Dr. McKenzie himself says, "the 'empirical' method, with its reliance on 'direct observation,' might lead us wildly astray" (p. 50).

But I must conclude. Dr. McKenzie's article is brilliant and he does offer much-needed warnings which we ignore at the peril of our study. How right he is in saying, "bibliography might grow the more securely if we retained a stronger assurance of its hypothetical nature" (p. 61). My quibbles are but quibbles. The serious weakness of his attack is, I suspect, not the trivial inconsistencies that strike me, but the basic misunderstanding of human nature and the study of bibliography that are implicit in the recommendation that salvation might be won "by pursuing the study of printing history to the point where analysis can usefully begin, or by returning – and this is the paradox – to the more directly useful, if less sophisticated, activity of enumerative 'bibliography'" (p. 61), and especially to the production of an STC or Wing for the eighteenth century.

Of course we must find out what we can of printing history – indeed have not we been trying to do just that? We must do it better and use our findings more carefully. It seems to me foolish to imagine that we have not learned a great deal about sixteenth-century printing house practices in the past ten or twenty years. But to imagine we can recover all is to pursue an *ignis fatuus*. Surely one problem that editors face is that all *cannot* be recovered. Even if we knew everything about printing house practices, we should still lack much that will never be recoverable of what underlay those practices; thus the editor will still be forced to conjecture. To deny the human urge to do something about the question which Erasmus posed to Martin Dorp in 1515 regarding different versions of the Bible is to misunderstand a basic characteristic of human nature:

> Postremo quid dicturi sumus, vbi viderimus nec huius aeditionis exemplaria consentire?

> What are we to say when we see that the exemplars of
> this edition do not agree?[5]

Since the seventh century B.C. when, it is suggested, men compared the different readings they found in texts on bricks from Ur, Lagash, and Babylon,[6] to the modern newspaper-reader who puzzles out a jumbled line of type, men have tried to answer the problem of the differences and corruptions in texts as best they can – even if such differences might seem no more than a Manichaean plot lacking the support of any corrupt copies, as St. Augustine suspects in *The Confessions* (Book 5, ch. 11). I cannot imagine that the errors we make will cause us to abandon that quest even if we can never be certain whether it is sullied or solid, eelskin or elfskin, or something totally different. Even if we do solve one problem in one place it will not necessarily advance us much further elsewhere. Years ago there was proposed a theory of continuous copy; it was then abandoned. A few years ago I actually discovered and reported physical examples of continuous copy in the work of Thomas Milles.[7] But though this is of interest regarding Milles, though it tells us more about one particular printing process, will it necessarily solve any of our other problems? Perhaps, however, we *are* learning, if slowly, for I know of no one who has yet generalized a further theory of continuous copy from this single author's work!

Bibliography attempts to work with two of the most worthwhile and most perplexing of variables: human beings and literature. The laws of logic apply to neither. We must continue to strive to push back the moment when we have to make our conjectures – when the guessing must begin – and we ought to be careful when we guess, that our guesses do not slip into seeming facts; but it is surely farcical to imagine, after nearly 3,000 years of unsuccessful inquiring, that the exposure of further errors over procedures will cause the human urge to discover, to guess what an author meant, to suddenly wither and die.

[5]*Opus Epistolarum Des. Erasmi Roterdami*, ed. P. S. Allen (Oxford, 1910), II, 111.
[6]W. P. Shepard, "Recent Theories of Textual Criticism," *MP*, XXVIII (1930), 129.
[7]*The Library*, Fifth Series, XVI (1969), 133-39.

The Contributors

BERNARD BECKERMAN, Professor of Dramatic Arts and Chairman, Theatre Arts, Columbia University. Author of *Shakespeare at the Globe, 1599-1609* and of several articles on theatrical history and dramatic theory.

PETER DAVISON, Senior Lecturer in English Language and Literature, University of Birmingham. Editor of several Elizabethan and Jacobean texts and author of articles on sixteenth and seventeenth century bibliography.

R. A. FOAKES, Professor of English, University of Kent at Canterbury. Editor (with R. T. Rickert) of *Henslowe's Diary* and author of many books and articles on the Elizabethan and Jacobean drama.

J. A. LAVIN, Professor of English, University of British Columbia. Editor of several Elizabethan plays and author of articles on sixteenth and seventeenth century bibliography.

TREVOR LENNAM, Professor of Drama, University of Calgary. Author of several articles on the Elizabethan drama.

LISE-LONE MARKER, Assistant Professor, Graduate Centre for the Study of the Drama, University of Toronto. Author of several articles on theatrical history.

D. F. ROWAN, Professor of English, University of New Brunswick. Author of several articles on the Elizabethan theatre.

S. SCHOENBAUM, Professor of English, Northwestern University. Editor of *Renaissance Drama* and author of many books and articles on the Elizabethan and Jacobean drama.

Index